The
Architecture
of Frank Williams

The Architecture of Frank Williams

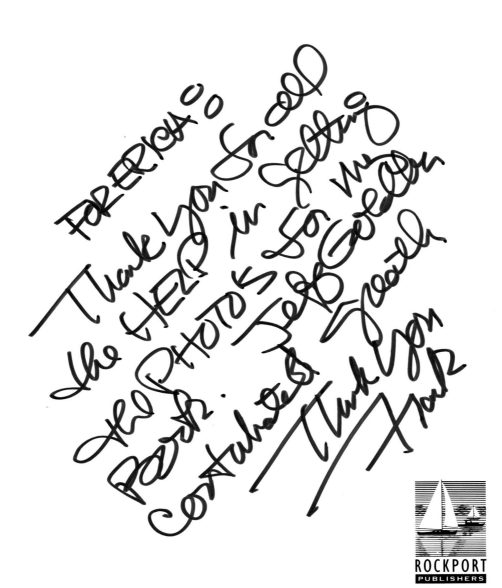

FOR ERICHA ?

Thank you for all the HELP in getting the PHOTOS for my Book. Sef God Bless. Congratulations graech

Thank you

Frank

ROCKPORT
PUBLISHERS

Rockport Publishers
Rockport, Massachusetts

Michael J. Crosbie

First published in the United States of America by:
Rockport Publishers, Inc.
146 Granite Street
Rockport, Massachusetts 01966-1299
Telephone: (508) 546-9590
Fax: (508) 546-7141

Distributed to the trade by:
Consortium Book Sales & Distribution, Inc.
1045 Westgate Drive
Saint Paul, MN 55114
(612) 221-9035
(800) 283-3572

ISBN 1-56496-305-5

10 9 8 7 6 5 4 3 2 1

Graphic Design: Lucas H. Guerra,
Argus Visual Communication, Boston

Cover Photograph: Jock Pottle/Esto

Printed in Hong Kong by
Regent Publishing Services Limited

CONTENTS

FOREWORD

ALEXANDER KOUZMANOFF, FAIA

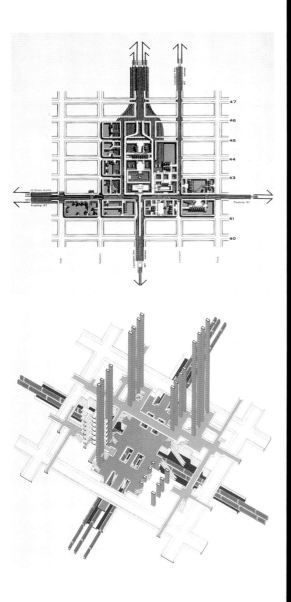

I first met Frank Williams in 1968 at a Regional Plan Association exhibition at the Architectural League in New York. The show was a large, interdisciplinary team study of mid-Manhattan directed by Frank Williams and Rai Okamoto, which resulted in their co-authored book, *Urban Design Manhattan*. The book had an immense impact on architectural offices and academic studios. The design method of organizing movement, systems, pedestrian interconnection, and the systems superimposed were beautifully and imaginatively illustrated. The study introduced an inspiring methodology for revitalizing and renewing the urban core, instead of the destructive and disruptive removal of urban cores taking place in so many American cities. The models presented were thought provoking. I asked Frank to join me as a studio critic to further explore his ideas with the Columbia University School of Architecture students.

He was an inspiring and an innovative teacher. Although he enjoyed the academic experience, he preferred building to creating studio projects. And build he did, for the next 25 years, here and abroad. He worked as an urban designer with large, interdisciplinary teams for projects in San Francisco, Philadelphia, New York, and a new community of 6,000 dwelling units and a town center for Teheran, Iran. In 1980 Williams opened his own practice in New York, focusing on hotels, urban residential, and mixed-use commercial buildings. With his rich background in urban design, he developed an architectural design vocabulary that expressed, both internally and externally, a talent for humanizing high-rise structures within their urban context. Precision, clarity, and elegance are a passion in Williams's approach to design. He understands the interplay of the horizontal forces of plan and the vertical forces of mechanics and structure. Working within the parameters established by real-estate marketing and zoning as well as the fluctuating marketplace, he manages to evoke the enduring qualities of massing and aesthetics that one associates with the elegant residential buildings in New York before the monolithic slabs took over in the 1950s. He was not

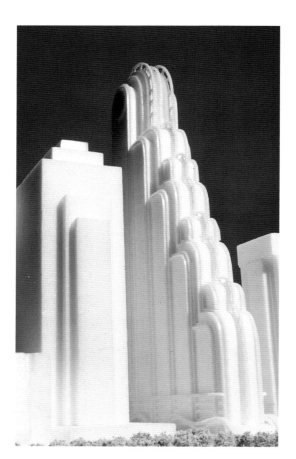

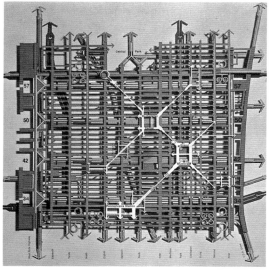

architectural offices. Jerry Goldberg and Tom Aidala of SOM developed an architectural design methodology for Market Street East, Philadelphia, that was an important lesson for me in how to structure a large, urban, mixed-use complex. Adding to this organizational experience was the architectural design work done in Teheran, where the important influences were Peter Wendt's emphasis on designing for cultural differences, and how best to understand these cultural differences.

Another wonderful experience and major influence on my architectural design has been working with major real-estate developers in New York like Bill Zeckendorf. He has taught me that each complex or each building must give some amenity back to the city, whether the zoning codes require this amenity or not. In other words, there is a civic responsibility underlying each private architectural commission undertaken in our cities today.

The collaboration on the Four Seasons Hotel in New York with I. M. Pei truly was a learning experience. His concern not to join architectural trends, but rather to make sure that modern-day architecture adheres to timeless design principles, has been a great influence on my design philosophy. My lasting friendship with I. M. also has been a wonderful opportunity to explore and learn from him the principles and experiences that shape his architecture.

Donald Trump's great enthusiasm and energy have shown me how much focus and dedication of one's life it takes to build an important building.

Aubrey Ferrao, our client in Florida, is teaching us that through architectural design, we can build for the future without losing some important human needs—such as a sense of permanence in our environment as well as a feeling of identity in the physical environment.

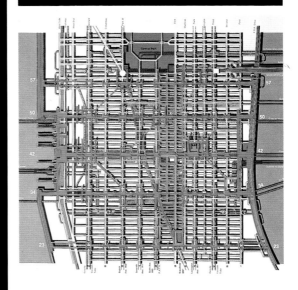

Suthipong Chirathivat, with whom we have three major buildings under construction in Bangkok, has renewed my belief that a Western architect can assimilate the values of a different country.

INTRODUCTION

MICHAEL J. CROSBIE

It is with a certain irony that we end the twentieth century with a resurgence in the architectural movement that ushered this century in, namely Modernism. But where the Modernism of a century ago presented the hope of a new machine age, an era of plenty, ease, and social harmony, the Modernism that closes the millennium is one wiser about architecture's limitations. While early Modern architecture came to represent some of the worst excesses of our age—the squandering of the earth's resources, the loss of the value of place, and the eradication of local culture and custom—Modern architecture today helps to mend those ways. Here, I am not referring to Modernism as style—that fetish for flash, glass, and impaling form that litters architectural magazines. Instead, I mean an attitude toward design that is Modern—the very best of a Modern way of thinking about technology in the service of humankind, about architecture engaged with the world as it exists (wherever it may be) and concerned with making people's lives better. Is this too simple a notion of Modern architecture? Is it too nostalgic or naive about the great manifestoes that young Modern architects pronounced seventy-five years ago? I hope not. For if it is, I don't see why anyone should give a damn about what we as architects do.

I believe that Frank Williams is a Modern architect of this stripe. He is a Modern architect who embodies what Sigfried Giedion articulated in *Space, Time, and Architecture*, when he wrote that Modernism was truly an international architecture that could capture and articulate what was special in a culture, special to a place, and special to people. It was only after Modernism became the International Style that things went rapidly and depressingly downhill. The International Style was everything that Giedion believed Modernism not to be: a pattern-book style, a one-size-fits-all architecture that obliterated the spirit of a place, raising its skirt above pilotis, to touch down in identical fashion in Toronto, Tbilisi, or Timbuktu.

The issues of space and time occupy us today because of the way it is possible to practice architecture.

Technology turns us into space and time travelers, and this is a new reality for architects to grapple with. When an architect such as Frank Williams travels with relative ease to design a building in Bangkok, or Berlin, or Beijing, to do his best he must accommodate the local values, the climate, the level of technology, and the mythology of the place. The compression of time and place challenges the architect not to take the easy route, not to stamp out his buildings as if with a cookie cutter. But there are conflicting forces at work. As Western architects recently have come to understand the mistakes of Modern architecture over the past fifty years, Eastern clients now ask them for Modern architecture in all its horrific detail as an expression that they, too, are part of the First World. How can the architect honor this request, without feeling as though he is delivering to his client the worst that we have to offer, only because it has come to symbolize Modern society?

Frank Williams sidesteps this trap by approaching design not as the manufacture of symbol (although that is what many of his clients seek, both in America and abroad), but as an expression of place that touches the subconscious identity of a city or a region. This requires a certain romantic view of architecture as a setting in which human life is to be played out, a value no doubt cultivated under the wing of Charles Moore, with whom Williams studied at Berkeley. For Moore, architecture's first duty was as a dream catcher, a place where memory could be cultivated and where it could repose—dreams and memories that are the very building blocks of human character and identity.

In his own buildings, Williams unearths the subconscious images that make us feel at home—that we identify with place—and incorporates these into his design. For example, in the design of the Four Seasons Hotel in New York—on which he collaborated with I. M. Pei—Williams has created a homage to one of the city's great cultural and architectural landmarks: Raymond Hood's RCA Building at Rockefeller Center. The tower of the Four Seasons rises with the same drama, peeling back layers as

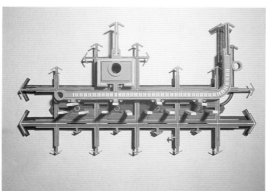

it reaches into the clouds. Its exterior material of limestone is brought into the lobby to give the space the stature of a monument, an immovable sense of place that memories of one's first trip to New York are made of.

Half a world away in Bangkok, Williams's design for The Terrace captures some of the same sense of defiant Modernism found in the Four Seasons, but delivers it with an Asian flavor. Bangkok's traditional architecture and its tropical, river-delta climate inspired the building's lacy texture. Many of the region's buildings have a rich basket-weave of trellises and screens, and this building captures that quality not in a literal way, but through such Modern materials as concrete. Balconies and terraces hover over the building and act as shading devices to help cool the building and filter the intense sunlight. The windows are set deeply into the building's frame, protecting them from sun and rain and promoting cross-ventilation. The building's stepped profile permits double-height spaces at the exterior of some of the apartment living spaces, encouraging airflow and ventilation and mitigating direct heat gain. But The Terrace is not a "themed" skyscraper à la Disney. Its materials and construction systems are Modern, with clean lines and structural expression. The Terrace shows how Williams infuses his buildings with a Giedion Modernism, responsive to their local condition yet clearly the product of contemporary technology, the very image that Asian clients wish to convey.

Williams believes that such an international practice, an opportunity to build around the world as a global architect, would not be possible without modern-day technology. He refers to CADD as an international language, a kind of architectural Esperanto that allows drawings to be translated over a thin phone wire, spirited around the globe to one's collaborators. Computers allow notes on drawings to be easily translated and printed in either English or Chinese, for example. A question from an associate at an engineering firm in Bangkok is easily resolved with a sketch that is faxed to New York, marked up, and faxed back. Like other architects on this cutting edge, Williams's practice runs virtually 24 hours a day. As the West sleeps, the East builds.

Working abroad also affects Williams's design of projects within a few blocks of his midtown office (the firm occupies one of the wonderful studios in Carnegie Hall, available only to those in the performing arts, which architecture qualifies as because "building" is also an action). Williams says that the advances in technology that have made his global practice possible have driven down overhead costs, making the firm more productive overall. Working abroad forces the architect to reconsider the careful organization and communication of information, which results in better construction documents and fewer change orders.

As architecture truly has become international, it forces a harsher light on the ravages of the International Style. We have seen the destruction of place with carpet-bombing design. We have seen the arrogance of technology in hermetically sealed buildings that consume far more natural resources than they need to. Frank Williams understands that a Modern architecture that is truly global can fulfill its role as a symbol of our age without sacrificing what makes it special to its neighborhood. In a time of great flux, uncertain transition, and shifting value—all as transient as electronic data on a hair-thin wire—global architecture as Frank Williams creates it gives us welcomed mooring.

Michael J. Crosbie
Essex, Connecticut

RIHGA ROYAL HOTEL

NEW YORK, NEW YORK

This fifty-four-story, all-suite hotel—the tallest in midtown Manhattan when it was completed—contains 514 suites, with no single rooms, making it unique among New York hotels. Its ground-level public spaces are scaled to be intimate, in the tradition of European hotels.

The most compelling aspect of the Rihga Royal's architecture is its presence in the city. The hotel's articulated tower form recalls the New York skyscrapers of the 1920s and 1930s. For the architect, the Rihga Royal is first and foremost a building about Manhattan's history and context. Although it does not pay homage to any one skyscraper in particular, it suggests a tradition of building in New York—through its materials and form—that most New Yorkers and visitors love about the architecture of the city.

The Rihga Royal's textured façade undulates for practical reasons. The tower is in the middle of a Manhattan block, with a tall office building directly across the street. The bay windows not only provide a wonderful vertical scale element, but open up the hotel suites to sunlight and views up and down 54th Street as well as give the tower its faceted form. All of the corners of the hotel's tower are chamfered to enhance the sculptured quality of the building's form and to provide a rhythmic pattern in harmony with the bay windows.

The two top floors of the hotel are dedicated to variously sized banquet rooms for meetings and receptions, and offer panoramic views of Manhattan. The Rihga Royal has a crenelated crown that gives it identity in the overall cityscape.

Rising from a granite base, the Rihga Royal's rose-colored brick mass states "this is a masonry tower" in a city of masonry landmarks, demonstrating how form and materials can help connect a building to the city's history.

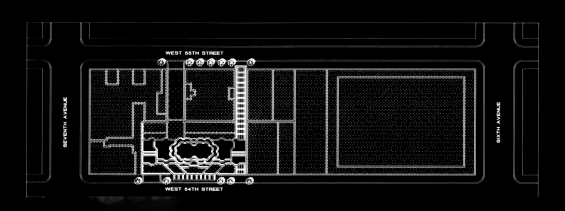

Right: Rear model view of hotel tower.

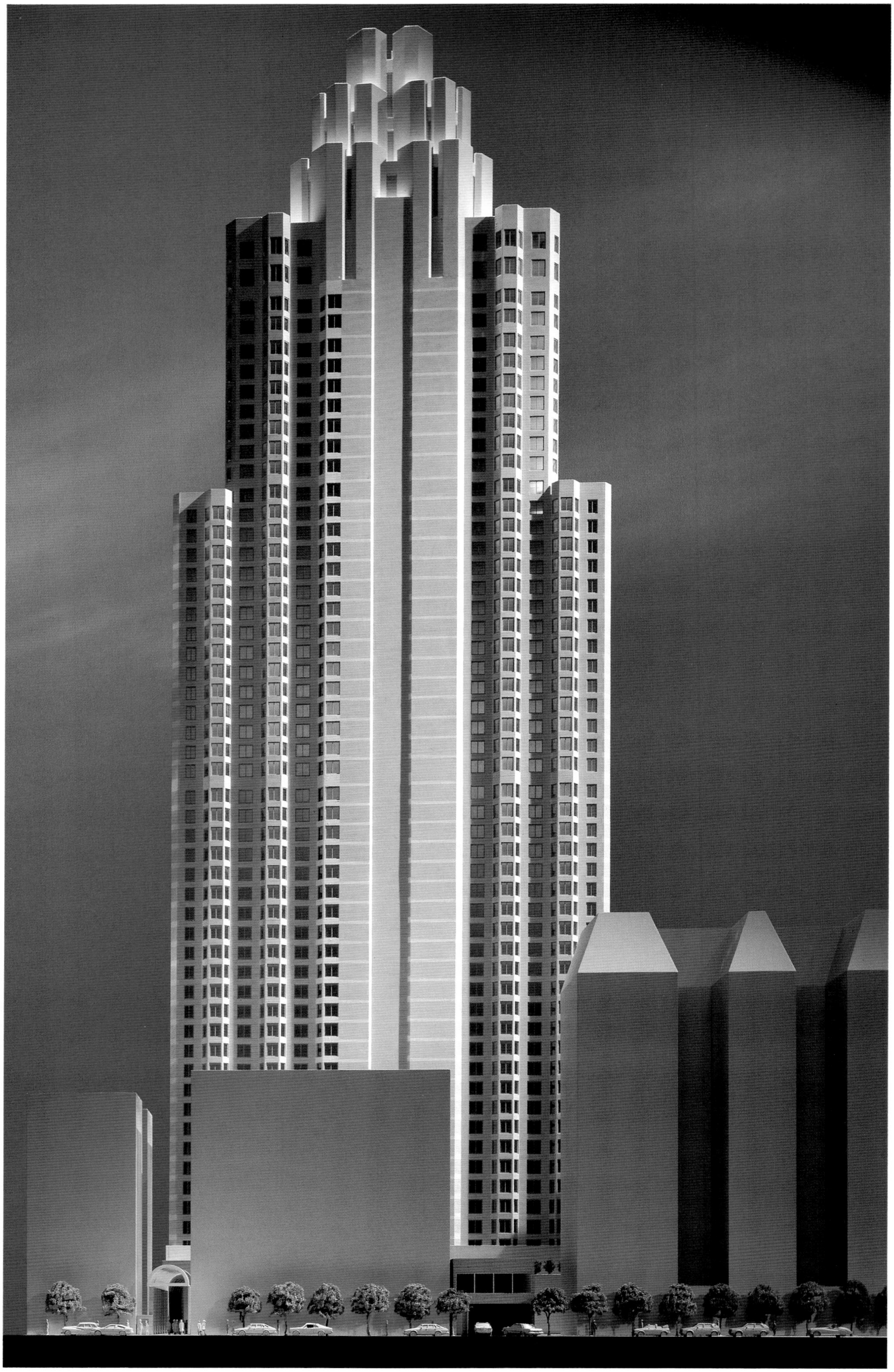

Left: Frontal model view of hotel tower.

Top: Bar on the 53rd floor has its own lounge.

Center: Elevator lobby on the 50th floor serves the banquet room.

Bottom: Banquet rooms on the 53rd and 54th floors are joined by an elegant public staircase.

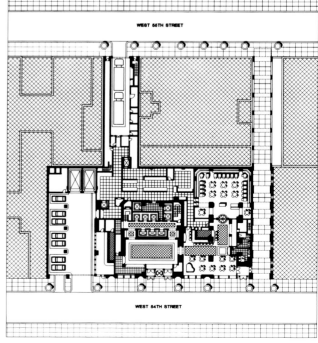

Ground Level Plan

Right: View from sidewalk
of West 54th Street accentuates the tower's bays.

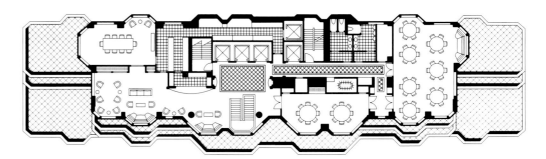

Meeting and Banquet Room Plan

Larger Suite Floor Plan

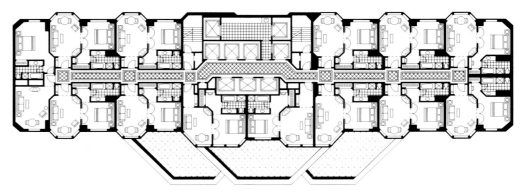

Typical Suite Floor Plan

Top: Gold ceiling and mahogany-paneled walls give space a rich appointment.

Center: Main restaurant is distinguished by a painted mural ceiling in European fashion.

Bottom: Bar and lobby lounge has an intimate scale.

Opposite Page: Second-floor foyer serves various meeting rooms.

Opposite Page: View from the bedroom to the living room in typical suite.

Top: Mirrored French doors separate living room from bedroom in typical suite.

Center: View into dining room from living room of two-bedroom suite.

Bottom: Bathrooms are elegantly appointed in marble in typical suite.

WORLD WIDE PLAZA

NEW YORK, NEW YORK

On the site of the old Madison Square Garden, World Wide Plaza is truly a unique architectural design opportunity in that this multi-use complex occupies a complete New York City block. Frank Williams is the architect for the Residential Complex and Skidmore Owings & Merrill are the architects for the Office Building.

The 2.5-million-square-foot complex has a rich mixture of uses ranging from the forty-nine-story office building to the thirty-eight-story residential tower and five-story town houses. Shops line the avenue, as is the tradition in New York, and at the center of the block is a park designed as the focus for the entire neighborhood. Movie theaters, restaurants, shops, and health clubs all surround the park and promote both day and evening activities.

Frank Williams designed the 660 World Wide Plaza residences to offer a variety of ways in which to live—a New York tradition. This wide range of living styles includes the thirty-eight-story tower with great views, the five-story town houses that line 49th and 50th Streets—which have their own stoop entrances along the side streets—and the private courtyard garden apartments. The thirty-eight-story mid-block residential tower is in scale with the office building, while the lower five-story town house apartments are integrated into the existing five-story fabric of the Clinton Historic Landmark District.

Paul Goldberger in *The New York Times* wrote of this project, "The residential design by Mr. Williams reflects the scale of the surrounding Clinton neighborhood. The design of World Wide Plaza, unlike that of so many other mega-projects, strengthens all four streets that it faces."

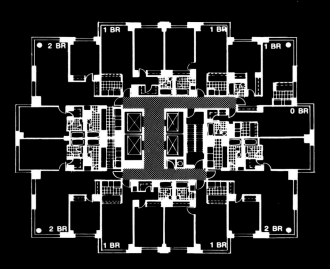

Floor Plan

Previous Page: Northwest view of apartment and office complex.

Right: View from the southwest; smaller tower contains apartments, while offices occupy larger tower.

Right: From the Hudson River, smaller residential towers help emphasize the scale of office tower.

Opposite Page: Residential tower and the low-scale housing capture all of the complexity of Midtown Manhattan, while holding the street space.

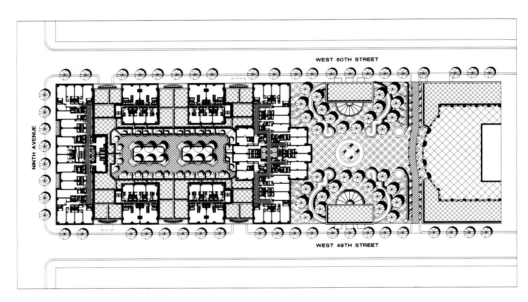

Typical Residential Courtyard Plan

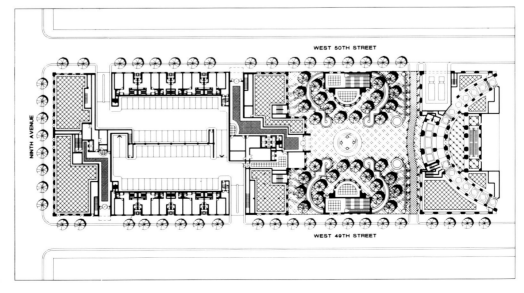

Ground Level Plan

Top: Middle of the residential block contains an oasis of garden space and light.

Center: Mid Block Plaza creates an appropriate foreground for the residential tower.

Bottom: Architectural details are in scale with public outdoor space.

Opposite Page: Residential tower and low-scale housing capture all of the complexity of midtown Manhattan.

Opposite Page, Top and Center: Rooftop terraces allow for outdoor living and dining.

Bottom: Low-scale buildings in the public square contain movie theater entrances.

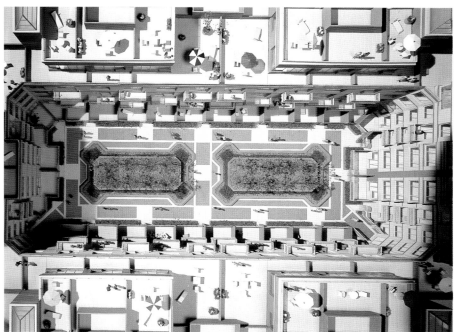

SHANGHAI INTERNATIONAL PLAZA

SHANGHAI, CHINA

This 1.4-million-square-foot office and shopping complex on Shanghai's waterfront represents the blossoming of China as a world financial power and is the result of an invited international competition. The development site is located near the Bund—a classical, historic, cosmopolitan district that faces the Huang Po River and was Shanghai's center in the 1920s. The Bund has many distinguished buildings punctuated with domes and spires, and at night their illuminated façades reflect along the waterfront.

Shanghai International Plaza takes its place along the southerly extension of the Bund in the form of three interlocking elements: two low-rise fourteen-story octagonal blocks that contain retail and office space, and a forty-five-story office tower that rises over a public plaza. The two lower elements complement the scale and mass of the existing classical buildings along the Bund, while the tower will be a new landmark on the Shanghai skyline.

Frank Williams chose the octagon form because of its prevalence in Chinese culture as a symbol of good fortune, which helps integrate the building into the local architectural tradition.

A plaza wraps the building at its base, offering a multi-level public realm that animates the development with street life. Near the tower's top are two observation decks with panoramic views of the city and the river. A fully glazed octagonal form containing three restaurants crowns the tower and appears as a large lantern. Smaller lanterns punctuate the tower and the low-rise buildings to meld them with the glowing landmarks along the Bund.

Shanghai International Plaza demonstrates that careful consideration of a region's architectural heritage, and attention to the existing structures along an important promenade, can result in a building that pays homage to the old while giving Shanghai a new, modern complex of buildings.

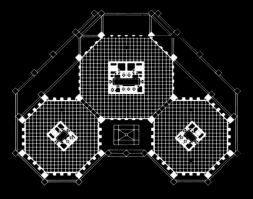

Typical Base Plan

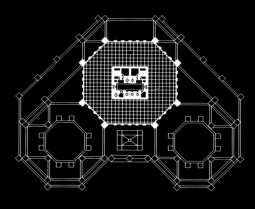

Typical Tower Plan

Previous Page: Lower
elements mediate tower's
scale with the street.

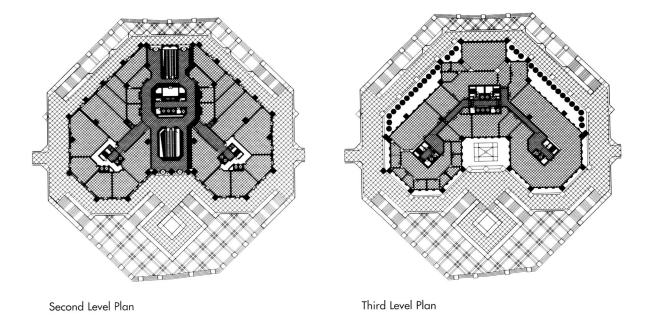

Second Level Plan   Third Level Plan

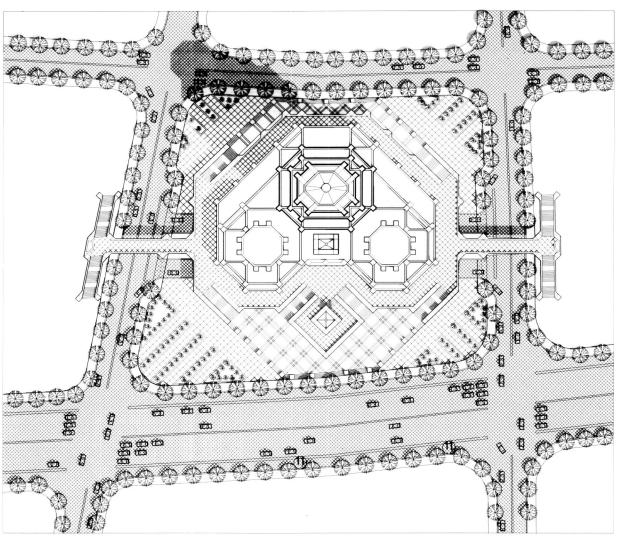

Site Plan

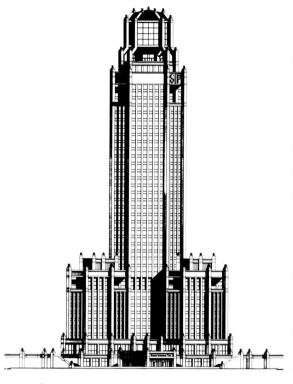

Front Elevation

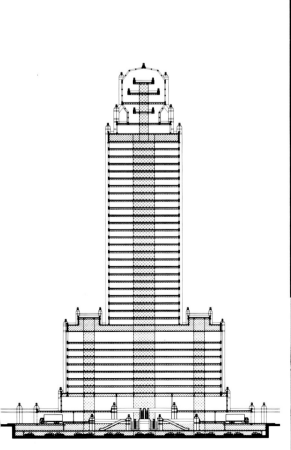

Building Section

Top: Model shows how tower rises out of low-rise base.

Bottom: Light sculpts tower and base so they appear cylindrical.

Top: Night view of the Bund shows the magic of lights and classical architecture that distinguishes this waterfront thoroughfare.

Center: Access to the upper promenade can be gained without entering building.

Bottom: Staircases, arcades, flags, and shopping on multi-levels give complex pedestrian vibrance.

Opposite Page: Top of the tower has a public observation level for views of the city and its waterfront.

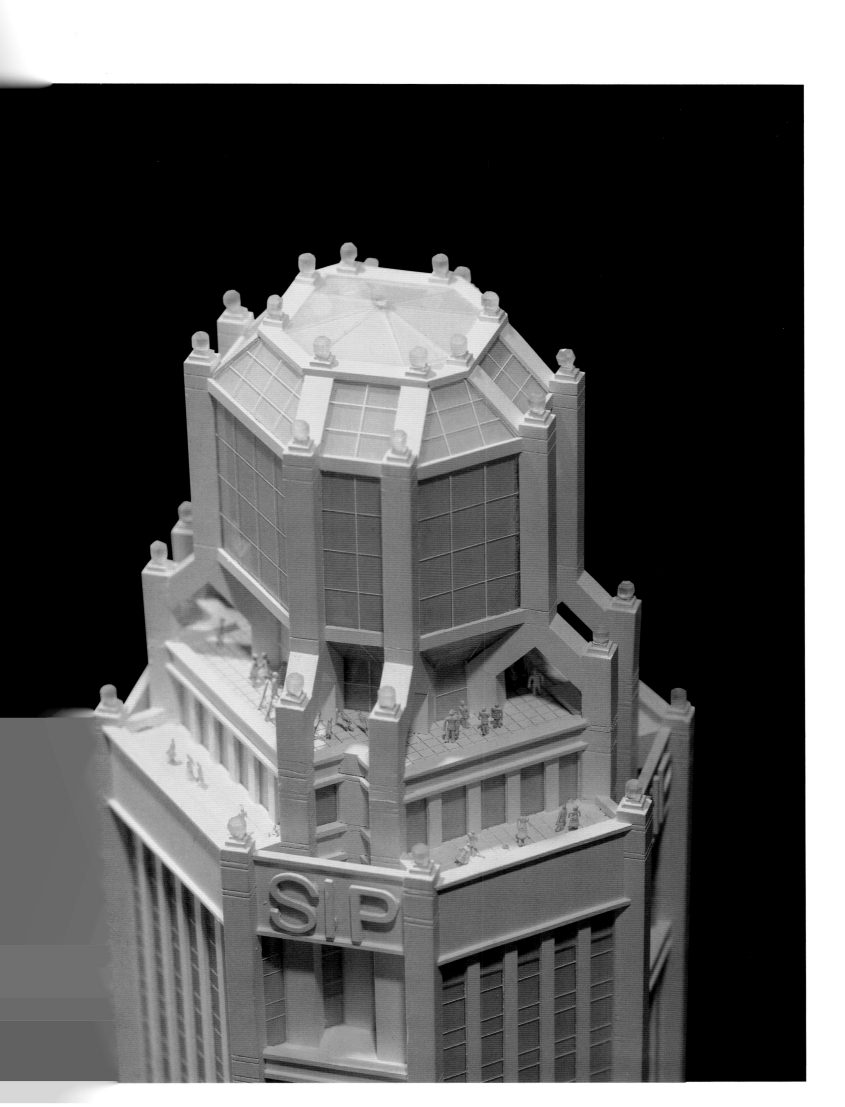

LANG SUAN VILLE

BANGKOK, THAILAND

Lang Suan Ville responds to the migration of people from the Asian Rim into the thriving city of Bangkok. This is the architect's first project in Thailand, and it represents a truly international collaboration of contractors, engineers, and consultants.

This 128-apartment residential tower takes its place on Lang Suan Road—a residential boulevard with the status of New York's Fifth Avenue along Central Park. The building faces a large, park-like area of Bangkok within which are found major embassies. Lang Suan Ville's stature, both as a place to live and as a high-rise, is accentuated by its adjacency to Bangkok's Lumpini Park.

Lang Suan Ville steps up in a series of setbacks that give an inviting scale to the architectural form, as do the solid corners that give the tower vertical emphasis. At the building's top is a pagoda-like structure

(screening mechanical equipment) that is similar to the traditional architecture found throughout Thailand. The building is constructed of a concrete frame over which a multi-colored tile is used that gives the exterior great precision and a beautiful matte finish.

Bangkok's climate is tropical year-round, and Lang Suan Ville's design reflects this in a two-layer exterior that provides shading for cooling and protection from the sun's glare. The building's stepped profile allows more corner spaces with operable windows for cross-ventilation. The tower is punctuated by deep balconies that provide shade and help to passively cool the building. Roof gardens, trellised terraces, and pools also respond to the climate and are important amenities in Bangkok's residential buildings. There are a health spa, on-site parking, and a variety of meeting rooms.

Elevation

Right: Rooftop pool is shaded by trellises overhead.

Typical Penthouse Unit Plan

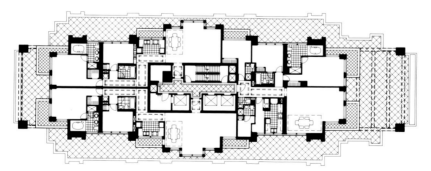

Typical Mid-Rise Unit Plan

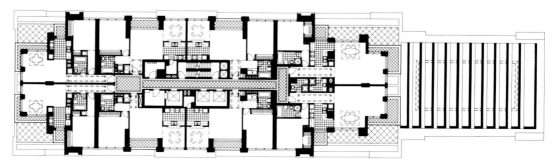

Typical Base Residential Plan

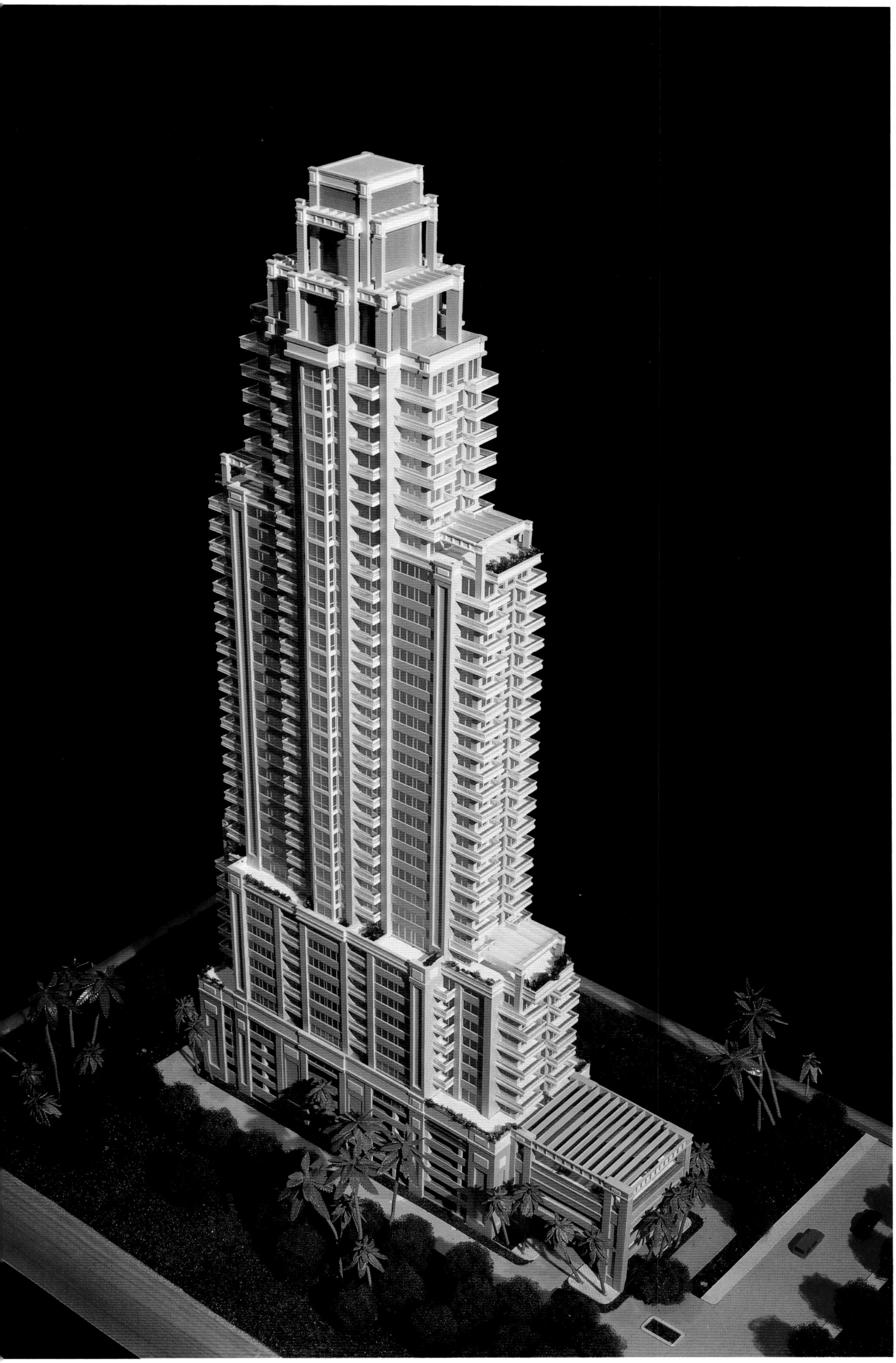

Left: Residential tower steps back from main thoroughfare.

Left: Residential tower in the context of Bangkok skyline.

THE BRITTANY

NAPLES, FLORIDA

This unique site offers water views in virtually every direction, as The Brittany takes advantage of its location in the design of its 121 condominiums. It also offers a variety of ways of living, from three-story private villas to garden apartments to tower suites to penthouses with wrap-around terraces.

The six private three-story villas create an entry into the Brittany complex, giving the development a comfortable scale along Gulf Shore Boulevard. One passes between the villa residences, with their private entries and garages at grade level and living spaces above, to arrive in a courtyard in front of the twenty-one-story tower. At this arrival level is a welcoming lobby with a library, meeting rooms, a billiards room, and guest salons. To the north and south of the lobby are four garden apartments.

Two tower apartments wrap around each of the three elevator cores on every floor, giving the apartments exposure to Venetian Bay on the east side and to the Gulf of Mexico on the west side. This arrangement allows apartments to take advantage of the prevailing cooling breeze, and limits the number of apartments per elevator tower to two, thus contributing to a sense of privacy. It also gives every apartment, each approximately 3,000 square feet, unobstructed views of the dramatic sunrises and sunsets, with large balconies east and west for outdoor living.

On the exterior, The Brittany's scale has been carefully modulated. Rising from the low scale of the three-story villas, the apartment block is articulated as three towers, with vertical bays accentuating the towers' height. Each tower gently steps back at the top and is crowned with a lantern. Lights at the towers' apex give The Brittany a glowing presence on the skyline. Colors of white and beige respond to the brilliant sunlight that is characteristic of this area.

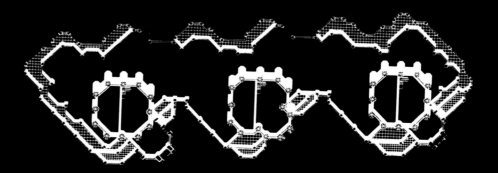

Roof Plan

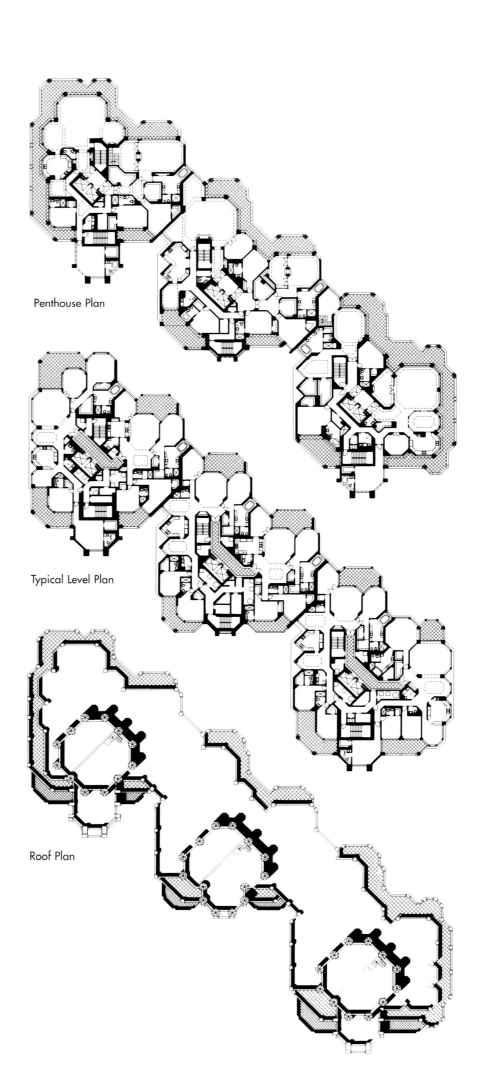

Penthouse Plan

Typical Level Plan

Roof Plan

Opposite Page: Towers culminate with sculptural crowns.

Top: Complex is sited with water views in a variety of directions.

Center: Site amenities include pool, spa, and health club.

Bottom: Lanterns at the top are complex sculptural elements that provide scale.

WAVE INTERNATIONAL TOWER

BANGKOK, THAILAND

In the thriving city of Bangkok, the Wave International Tower will rise on a site at the heart of the new financial district. Located on busy Ploenchit Road, the site is a long, rectilinear parcel of land surrounded by recently completed office buildings of steel and glass. Unlike many commercial structures in the city, this forty-five-story tower will be capable of handling the demanding loads of a state-of-the-art office building.

The cascading form of the office tower is reminiscent of other designs by Frank Williams that mediate between the scale of the city and that of the street. With a form that literally echoes the client's name, the tower gently cascades down in a series of dramatic curves. The base contains shops and restaurants.

The tower is completely clad in glass, giving it the appearance of a sensual wave. As the tower steps back from the street, it also reveals a series of layers that visually diminish the building's mass. The open-web steel tracks that race up the tower's centerpoint accommodate window-washing equipment.

For thermal comfort, the glass skin is shaded with a mechanical louver system that is located behind the glazing. This shading device responds to the sun's intensity and movement, automatically adjusting the blinds to modulate the interior climate and illumination. In his own words, Frank Williams describes the Wave International Tower as "a study of architectural form as a metaphor."

Building Elevation

Left: Tower's sculptural form cascades from the skyline to the street.

55

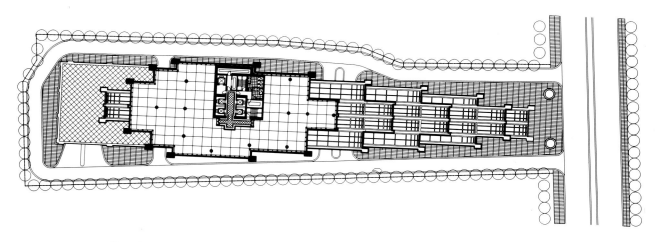

Typical High-Rise Office Plan

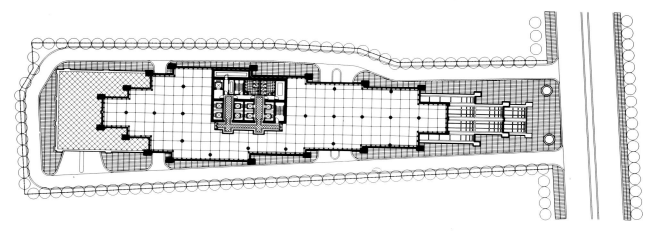

Typical Low-Rise Office Plan

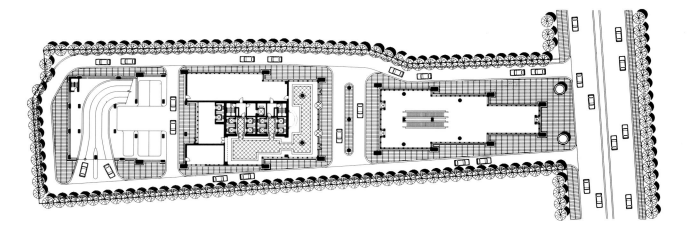

Site Plan at Grade Level

Left: Rising above adjacent buildings, the Wave Tower takes its place on the skyline.

THE GOTHAM

NEW YORK, NEW YORK

New York has a heritage of grand apartment buildings that date from the early decades of the twentieth century. These structures have distinctive profiles, sensitive human scale, and a classical tripartite organization of base, middle, and top. The Gotham expresses this heritage in its design, while offering most of the amenities needed for contemporary urban living.

The Gotham is located on Third Avenue between 86th and 87th Streets, in the heart of one of the city's best neighborhoods on the Upper East Side. This is an attractive neighborhood for young families who wish to live near some of the city's finest schools. Designed with families in mind, The Gotham contains 241 luxury residences, a large percentage of which have four bedrooms. At the base of the building is a variety of shops and restaurants to give it an active urban edge. Below-grade are seven movie theaters that are entered from Third Avenue. The residential condominiums are accessible from the main entrance on 87th Street. At a lower level are a pool and health spa for the residents.

The Gotham's form and articulation distinguish it as a New York building. It fills out the site with a street wall that is very characteristic of New York. This street wall has a cornice, above which are two stories that reinforce the cornice line. The eleven stories above the cornice step back with a gentle slope, creating terraces and a mansard-like profile.

At the very top is an octagonal lantern that anchors the building in its urban setting and houses a mechanical penthouse. The Gotham's tripartite division shows respect for the Park Avenue buildings that are part of this Upper East Side neighborhood. Its scale is modulated with two-story recessed balconies that suggest a smaller building than this actually is. The recesses also emphasize the façade's vertical lines, lending The Gotham a stature befitting its refined context.

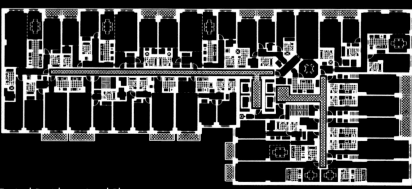

Typical Residence Level Plan

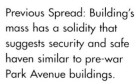

Previous Spread: Building's mass has a solidity that suggests security and safe haven similar to pre-war Park Avenue buildings.

Opposite Page: Sculptural tower top anchors the building on the skyline.

Top: On Third Avenue, the architectural form turns the corner in stepped two-story terraces.

Center: With midtown Manhattan in the background, building celebrates its urban context.

Bottom: Large balcony setbacks break down building's scale.

Right: First floor is dedicated to retail use.

Opposite Page: From the northeast, building has a commanding presence as it turns the corner.

EAST 87TH STREET

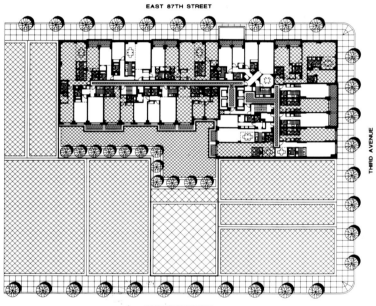

THIRD AVENUE

EAST 86TH STREET

Typical Residence Level Plan

EAST 87TH STREET

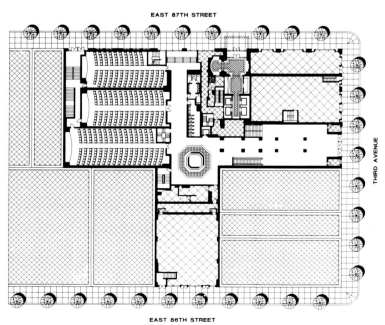

THIRD AVENUE

EAST 86TH STREET

Grade Level/Theater Level Plan

101 CALIFORNIA

SAN DIEGO, CALIFORNIA

This project demonstrates the care inherent in a global approach to design attuned to enhancing the context. The site for 101 California is at the very heart of San Diego, on the city's waterfront and at the starting point of Highway 101, which extends north for thousands of miles into Alaska. A mix of commercial and residential uses, the building takes the form of a forty-story tower, with three-story town houses serving as its base. Thus, 101 California simultaneously serves as a new landmark on the city's skyline and provides a lively block of pedestrian activity that weaves into a nearby residential neighborhood scale.

As befits its important urban site, the tower is oriented at a forty-five-degree angle so that it relates to the axis of Harbor Drive, one of the city's major thoroughfares. The corner site is defined by the eleven-story-high base that extends to the sidewalk's edge and relates to the scale of an adjacent hotel. The ground floor contains retail shops and restaurants. On the roof deck of this eleven-story block of one- and two-bedroom apartments are outdoor terraces, a swimming pool, and a health spa for use by the residents. Above this block rises the condominium tower, which is articulated as two spires, whose verticality is emphasized by bay windows and balconies that afford panoramic views of the city and the waterfront. To the west of the tower, the site opens up to a pedestrian promenade that is being designed by Alex Cooper. This carefully scaled public space is alive with outdoor dining, trees, shopping, and three-story town houses. A more private outdoor space is found in the heavily planted courtyard formed by the tower and the town houses, which offers residents a green oasis in the heart of downtown.

Town house units, animated with vine-covered trellises, balconies, awnings, and private garden spaces, provide an active edge and give the block the scale, color, and vibrancy of an intimate neighborhood. As architecture critic Dirk Sutro wrote of 101 California in *The Los Angeles Times*, "This project illustrates how dense high-rise development along the waterfront can make a positive contribution."

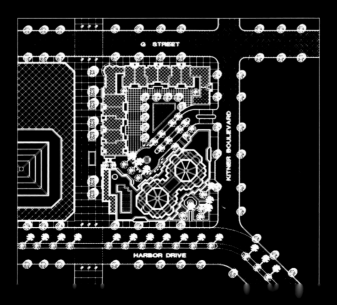

Previous Page: Between residential complex and an adjacent existing hotel is a pedestrian promenade.

Right: Base of the tower has swimming pool and health club opening onto the roof.

Opposite Page: Site has a courtyard garden between tower and town houses.

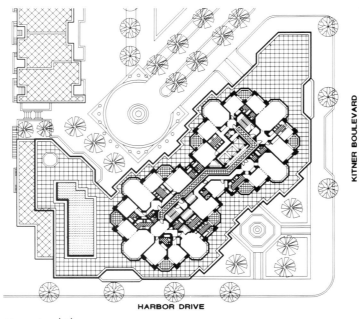

Upper Level Plan

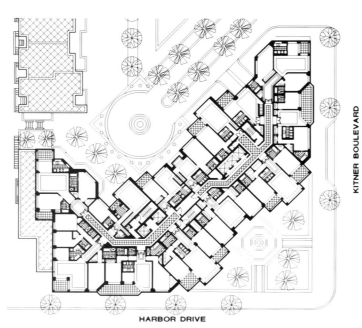

Lower Level Plan

TRUMP PALACE

NEW YORK, NEW YORK

Manhattan's great skyscrapers of the 1920s and 1930s, specifically those such as the Chanin Building and Rockefeller Center's RCA Building, are part of the city's architectural heritages to which Trump Palace pays homage. The distinguishing qualities of those buildings are that they are masonry-clad structures with punched, rectangular fenestration that is carefully scaled to the human body. They rise as stepped towers that become more sculptural as they touch the sky. The design of Trump Palace employs these design principles to give it a distinctive presence as the Upper East Side's tallest residential building, containing 383 luxury residences in a mixture of different housing types.

At grade level, Trump Palace occupies the depth of a city block, extending from 68th to 69th Street. The building meets the ground with a variety of shops, a public plaza, and town house residences. The next half-dozen floors contain studios and one-bedroom residences. From this dense low-rise block, which relates to the scale of the neighborhood context, the fifty-five-story tower rises in four sections that step back. The four walls of the tower are faceted in a fashion similar to the RCA Building, giving Trump Palace a layered appearance.

As the tower ascends, the apartments become larger, and within the top six stories they occupy the entire floor. At the top, crenelated planes of white and rose brick provide the tower with a distinctive crown. *The New York Times* architecture critic Herbert Muschamp praised Trump Palace as "a distinctive object: a rose-colored prism rising into the clouds."

Perspective View

Previous Page: Distinctive roof profile is in the same vocabulary of other New York buildings.

Right: At corner of 69th Street and Third Avenue, low-scale buildings mediate with the street.

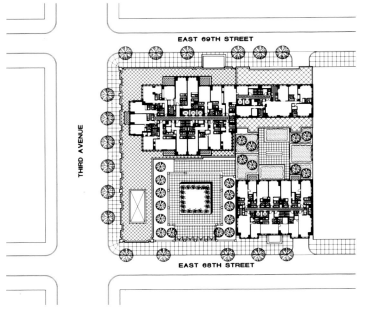

Lower Level Residential Plan

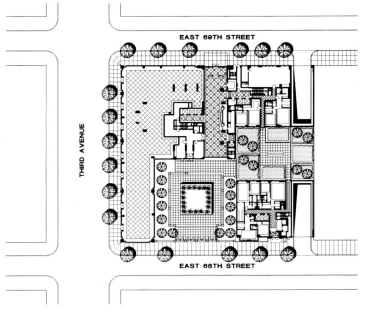

Ground Level Plan

Left: From East 69th Street, tower takes its place on the skyline.

Right: A corner detail reveals the combination of materials and colors.

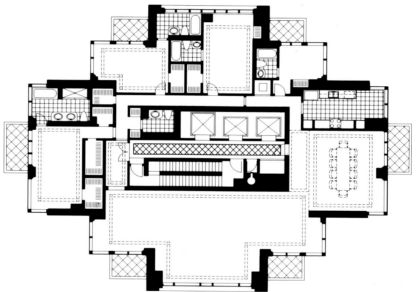

Penthouse Residential Floor Plan

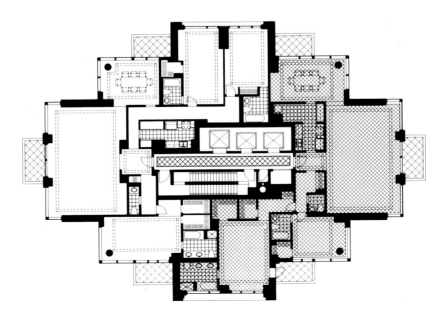

Upper Level Residential Floor Plan

Opposite Page: A lobby lounge overlooks the exterior courtyard.

Top: Residential lobby is detailed with mixture of wood and marble.

Bottom: View from low-rise wing elevator lobby to main lobby.

Four Seasons Hotel New York

New York, New York

Frank Williams describes his collaboration with I. M. Pei on the design of the Four Seasons Hotel (New York's tallest hotel) as an unparalleled learning experience. Many of the architectural design principles explored during this collaboration have been carried further in the design of other buildings, particularly in the Shanghai International Plaza.

In the heart of the city, the commanding location—57 East 57th Street, between Madison and Park Avenues—required a building design that would complement its surrounding environment. The architectural response to this important site has been to start with a street wall that is crowned with an oculus. The tower then steps back gracefully, echoing the form of another Manhattan landmark, the RCA Building at Rockefeller Center.

The New York tradition of punched windows in a strong masonry mass is used by the architects both to respect the adjacent Fuller Building and to tie into the fabric of the surrounding area. To emphasize the solidarity of the limestone, which was quarried in Magny, France, the corners of the hotel exterior are chamfered and extended to communicate a strong

sense of permanence, a sense that this building will be here for a very long time. The recessed quality of the tripartite, punched windows adds to the permanence of the building.

A series of public rooms connects this mid-block site between East 57th and East 58th streets. Starting from the 57th Street entrance, one arrives in the thirty-three-foot-high limestone foyer with its translucent onyx ceiling. Gracious stairs lead to the terraced lobby lounges on both sides. The hotel reception area is on axis with the coffered elevator lobby. Finally, split-level staircases lead up to a light and airy bar-restaurant level, or down to the 58th Street sidewalk entrance. These public rooms communicate a sense of place that one associates with great hotels of a generation or more ago—the Waldorf Astoria, for example.

Of this project, *New York* magazine commented that "I. M. Pei and associate architect Frank Williams's design should contribute mightily to the city's perception of itself as a seat of enlightenment and sophistication. It is a noble design, akin in spirit to Grand Central Terminal and the Chrysler Building."

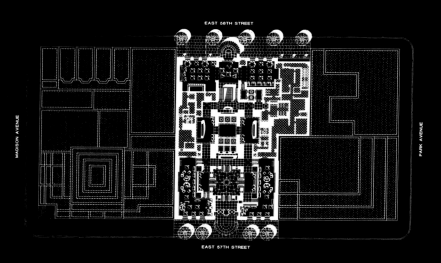

Ground Level Plan

Previous Page: Hotel tower rises over its midtown context and melds with it.

Right: Hotel tower occupies mid-block location on East 57th Street.

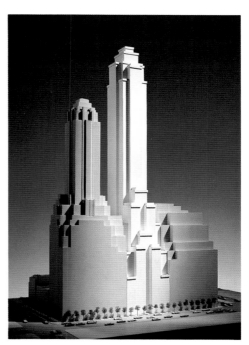

Top and Center: Massing studies reveal hotel's layered composition.

Bottom: Massing studies reveal hotel's layered composition and mid-block presence.

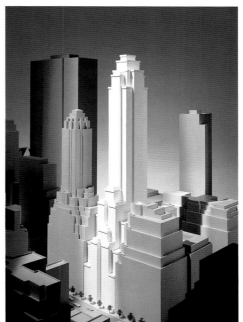

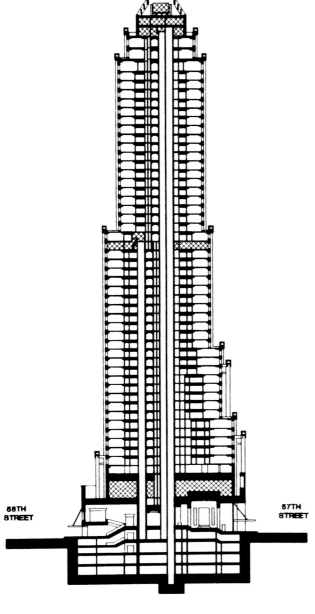

58TH STREET

57TH STREET

Building Section

Opposite Page: Hotel tower shows its layered, sculptural quality.

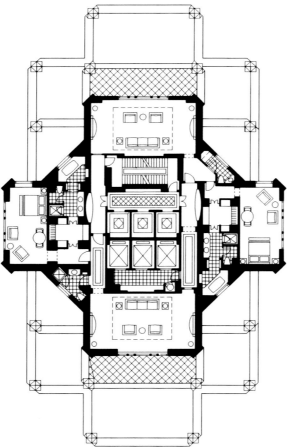

Upper Level Suite Plan

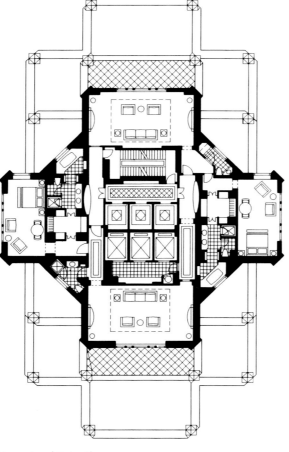

Presidential Suite Plan

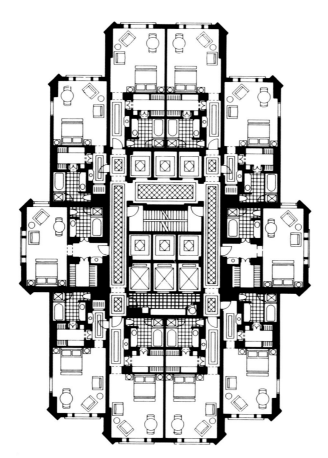

Typical Suite Plan

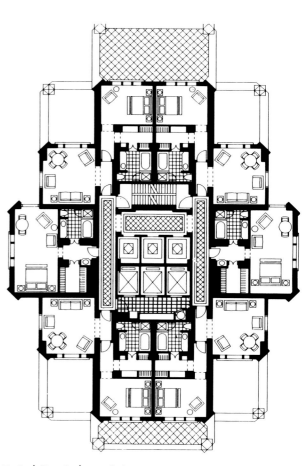

Typical One-Bedroom Suites

Opposite Page: With a view across from one of the many lounges, visitors can view the comings and goings of the hotel.

Top: Main reception desk has an air of restrained elegance and grandeur.

Bottom: Grand stair connects a restaurant on the upper level to the entrance from 58th Street.

Right: Typical suites have gracious living rooms.

Opposite Page: The Four Seasons Hotel is distinguished by its finely appointed bathrooms.

Top: Some rooms afford excellent views of Central Park.

Bottom: Meeting spaces on upper floors offer breathtaking views of the city.

THE TERRACE
BANGKOK, THAILAND

This thirty-story residential building in Bangkok responds to its rich context in a variety of ways. In scale, it is sympathetic to both the city skyline and street life. It provides welcome climate control strategies, and it incorporates elements of traditional Thai architecture that marry it to this regional context.

The Terrace residential tower is located on a site surrounded by urban residential buildings. Its height allows it to establish a presence in this context, while the building's stepped and layered form brings its mass down to a comfortable scale. At the base are an elegant lobby and on-site parking for 180 cars, above which are eighty-eight condominium residences. The design of this residential tower is oriented to families, with a large percentage of the apartments designed as four-bedroom units. The rooftop features an outdoor terrace, a health club and spa, and a swimming pool, which is a popular feature in this city of year-round warm weather.

Thailand's traditional architecture and its tropical river-delta climate inspired the building's fabric-like texture. Many of the region's buildings have a rich basket weave of trellises and screens, and this building captures that quality, not in a literal way, but through the use of trellises and interlocking rhythms of balconies and roof terraces. The shading devices help cool the building and filter intense sunlight. The windows are set deeply into the building's frame, protecting them from sun and rain and allowing for cross-ventilation. The building's stepped profile permits double-height spaces at the exterior of some of the apartments' living spaces, encouraging airflow and ventilation, and helps to mitigate direct heat gain. The building's concrete-frame structure, with concrete panel infill and white tile cladding, also helps to deflect the sun's heat and protect the interior spaces.

For Frank Williams, The Terrace represents an approach to global design that does not replicate traditional architecture, but interprets it in a Modern vein that will allow the new building to respond to and embrace its environment.

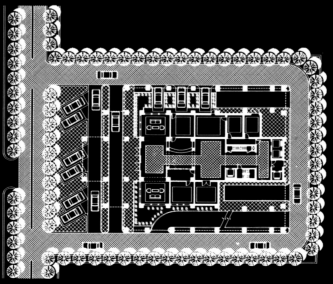

Ground Level Plan

Previous Page: Cascading form and rich texture relate to Bangkok's climate and culture.

Top: Stepped floors sculpt the building's form as light moves around it.

Center: Building has a basket weave of trellises, which suggest traditional architectural elements.

Bottom: Mass of the building is perforated by the trellised terraces.

Opposite Page: Stepped form gives the building a human scale.

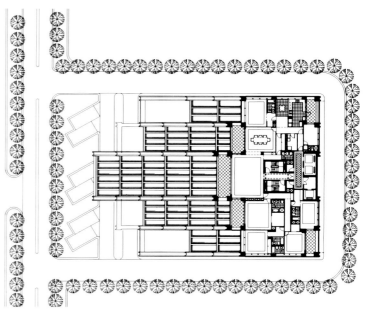

Upper Level Residential Plan

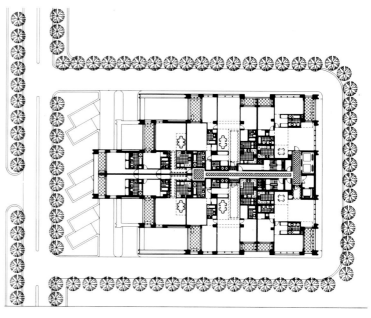

Lower Level Residential Plan

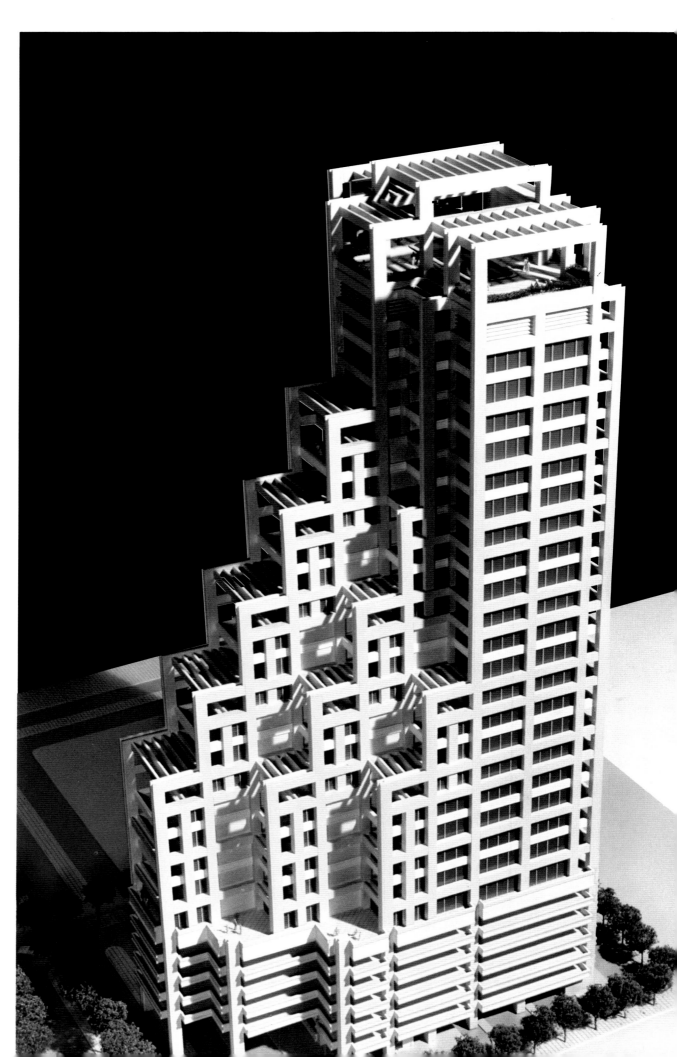

Right: Cascading form mediates between scale of the city and that of the street.

Setbacks allow outdoor living spaces for the residences.

THE PARK BELVEDERE

NEW YORK, NEW YORK

Manhattan has a great tradition of residential streets, and Central Park West is perhaps its most fashionable. Grand apartment houses rise along this boulevard, overlooking the city's greatest greensward. The Park Belvedere, a residential tower only a block west of the notable avenue, partakes of this tradition. This thirty-five-story building, comprising 155 luxury residences, rises above 79th Street and Columbus Avenue. The base of the building is a street wall that steps back. A trellised roof garden wraps the building. The tower culminates in a terraced silhouette.

This sculptural crown owes a debt to the towers that terminate the classic 1930s residential buildings along Central Park West, such as the San Remo and the Beresford. Like these majestic structures, the Park Belvedere is a masonry clad building with punched rectangular windows. To the east of the Park Belvedere

is one of the city's great cultural institutions, the American Museum of Natural History. The low-rise museum allows unobstructed views of Central Park from the Park Belvedere, and the museum's own park-like setting extends the view of treetops virtually to the building's front door. The Park Belvedere's rose-colored brick is respectful of the museum's brick color.

Inside, the apartments are spacious, featuring nine-foot ceilings, expansive living rooms with corner windows, and separate dining rooms. As a testimonial to the building's amenities, the developer, the contractor, and the architect call the Park Belvedere home.

Paul Goldberger wrote in *The New York Times*, "The Park Belvedere recalls the romantic silhouettes of the 1930s of the Central Park West skyline."

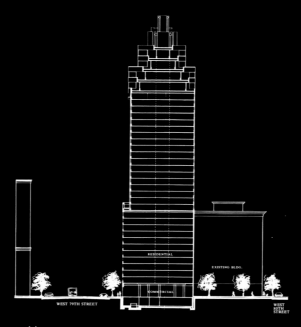

Building Section

Previous Page: Building as it faces park behind American Museum of Natural History.

Top: Building fills out its 79th Street site.

Center: Top of the building steps back to give it a distinctive profile that relates to context.

Bottom: View of the model from the southeast.

Opposite Page: Tower with its distinctive profile fits well into its Central Park West neighborhood.

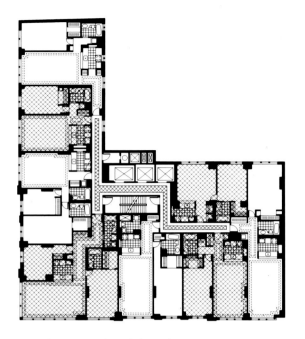

Typical Base Residential Floor Plan

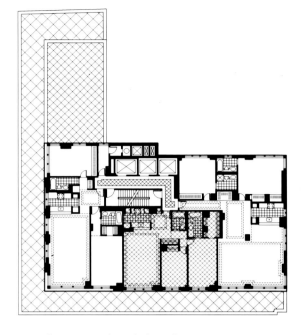

Typical Tower Residential Floor Plan

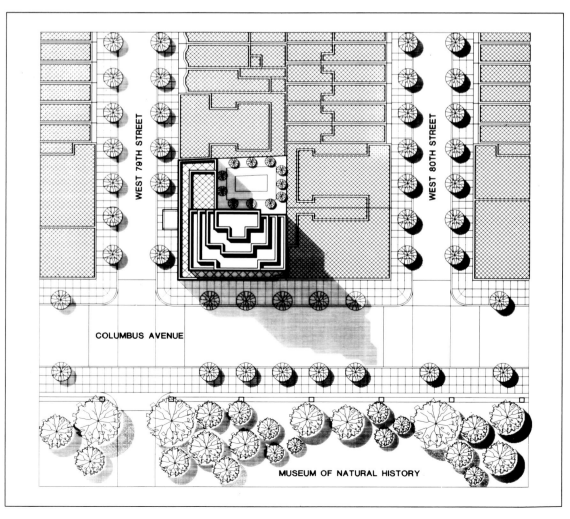

Site Plan

Left: Park Belvedere fits into the Central Park context.

Right: Aerial view of Park Belvedere shows how it relates to American Museum of Natural History.

BERLIN FRIEDRICHSTRASSE

BERLIN, GERMANY

This development was designed in response to an invited international competition, in collaboration with Moore Ruble Yudell Architects. The program involved the design of three entire blocks at the center of Berlin on the major shopping thoroughfare. To the east of the site is the nineteenth-century classical ensemble of the Platz der Akademie. The new development would contain shopping, offices, and a hotel—a rich combination of activities to bring this commercial site into a meaningful partnership with the adjacent cultural landmarks. Subway connectors below grade would tie the complex to the metropolitan city and provide the focus for this major destination in Berlin.

The volume of this infill project is governed by a seven-story height limitation which is respectful of the surrounding buildings. The design concept is to give full expression to the complexity of the program, and in particular to develop a sense of urban theater appropriate to this cultural, shopping, and office center—an elaborate stage for the arrival and movement of visitors and residents within the site. The solution takes the form of a series of celebratory public spaces that penetrate all three blocks, unified by scale. There is a variety of entries into the multi-block development from the surrounding corners and cross streets. The angled interior street, which functions as a grand promenade, is a dividing line between the blocks' myriad functions. Along Friedrichstrasse are retail spaces, knitting the block into this thoroughfare's tradition as one of Berlin's great shopping districts. To the east of the retail block, accessible from the promenade, are entrances to offices and the hotel. Distinctive sculptural elements throughout the development—such as glazed drums, gabled penthouses, and stepped cubes—serve as landmarks and unify the design. As it faces the surrounding context, the blocks are massed and rendered in materials that tie this development to the architectural traditions of this European capital.

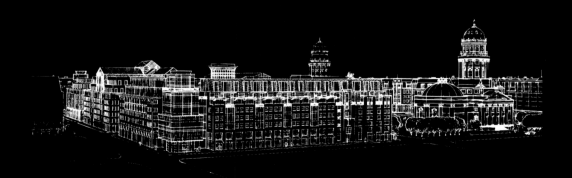

Perspective View

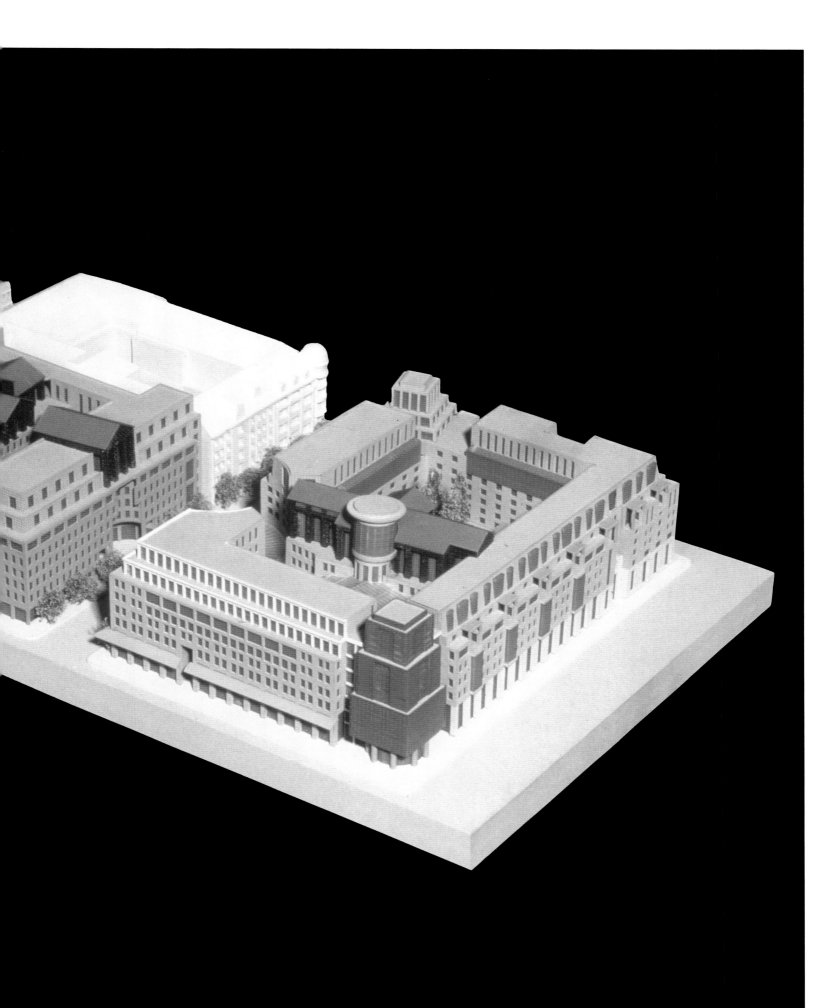

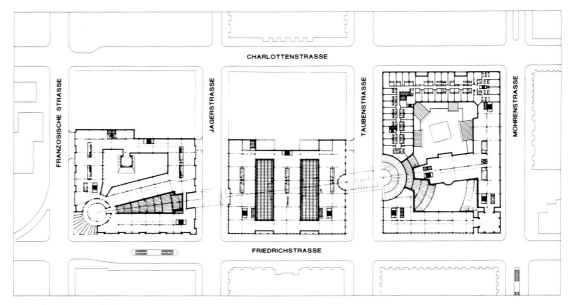

Typical Upper Level Plan

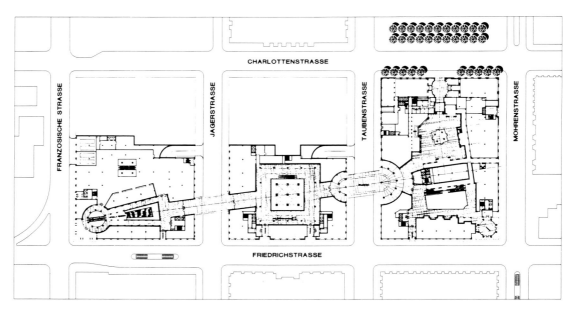

Ground Level Plan

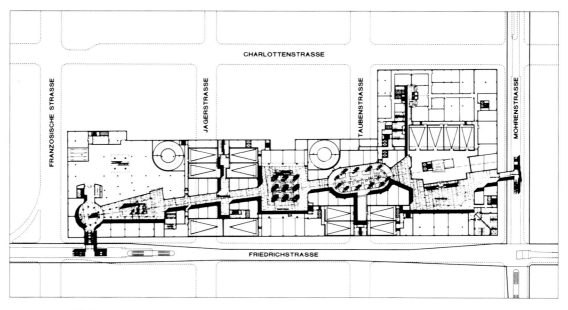

Basement Level Plan

Previous Page: Corners are celebrated with sculptural elements.

Left: Roofscapes are broken by landmarks, such as temple-like structures.

Following Page: Immediate context includes nineteenth-century Classical architecture.

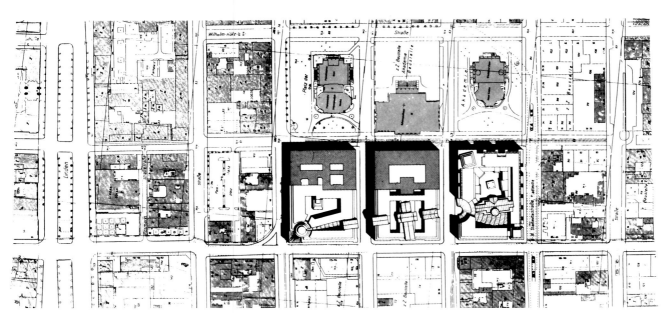

Site Plan

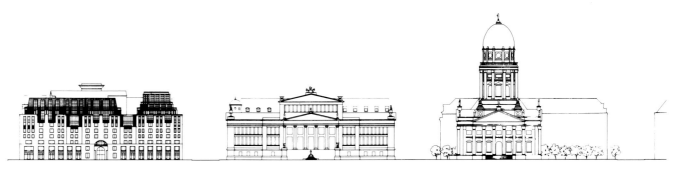

Mohrenstrasse Elevation

Friedrichstrasse Elevation

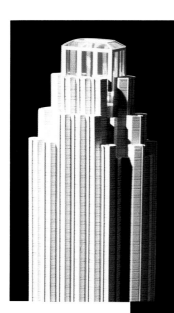

THE REGENT HOTEL
THE REGENT RESIDENCES

SHANGHAI, CHINA

As China opens to international trade and travel, providing accommodations for a new group of travelers has become critical. The Regent Hotel and Regent Residences are designed with this in mind, providing not only a world-class hotel but also residences for guests to live in for extended periods.

This preliminary master plan has been completed to evaluate a specific site located on Huai-Hai Road, one of Shanghai's most fashionable shopping and commercial thoroughfares. An additional master plan is being developed for a different site that is also on Huai-Hai Road.

The Regent Complex comprises two parts: a 400-room hotel tower and a lower-scaled residential tower of 200 service apartments. There are separate entrances and elevator systems for each of these functions. The two are linked at the site's most public corner. As the building turns the corner, the ground level opens completely to allow access into the site's park-like interior.

The fifty-story Regent Hotel includes a lobby lounge and a variety of meeting rooms, restaurants, and banquet rooms that are found on the second floor and at the very top, where a glass enclosure offers excellent views of the city. The tower itself is rendered as a faceted surface, using the bay windows in the hotel rooms to allow views up and down Huai-Hai Road. Frank Williams used a similar approach in his design of the Rihga Royal Hotel in New York, giving the tower a sculptural feeling, communicating a sense of the building's permanence.

The fifteen-story residential tower offers one- to three-bedroom service apartments for extended family living, complete with furnishings and the most up-to-date communication links such as faxes, phones, and computer terminals.

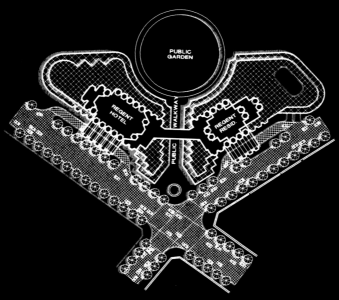

Site Plan

Previous Page: Adjacent public park creates an open foreground for the tower.

Opposite Page: Pathways allow circulation across the site to destinations beyond the block.

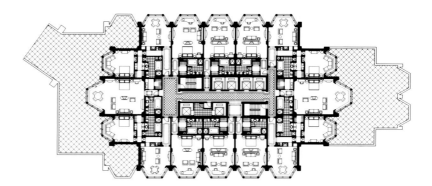

Residence Typical Floor Plan

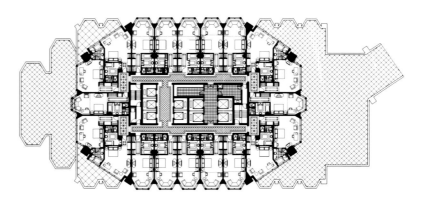

Hotel Typical Floor Plan

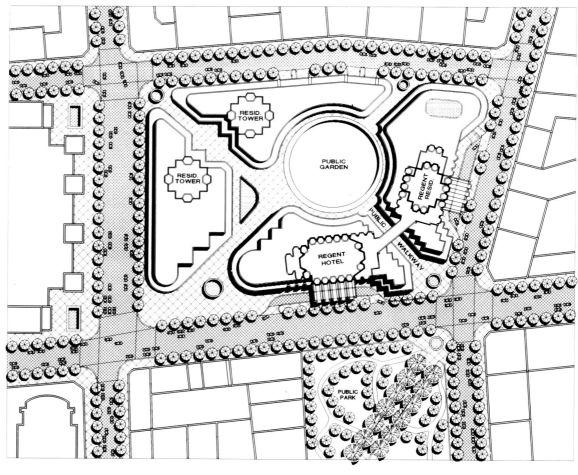

Site Plan

Opposite Page: Tower and residences have bay windows to enhance views from guest rooms.

Top: Lower-scale element next to the hotel contains residences for extended stays.

Bottom: Corner of the site is celebrated with a gateway to interior public garden.

SOUTH FERRY PLAZA

NEW YORK, NEW YORK

Modern New York City has never established a strong tie with its extensive waterfront. The city's major buildings have usually focused landward, toward uptown or Central Park, and rarely toward the rivers that ring Manhattan. The competition-winning design of South Ferry Plaza redresses that deficit. Sited at the very tip of the island at Whitehall Street, South Ferry's 1.5- million-square-foot tower rises as a beacon over Battery Park and New York Harbor.

The sixty-story tower at the heart of South Ferry Plaza is conceived by Frank Williams as "a metaphor of a lighthouse," its dome-shaped pinnacle fully glazed and illuminated at night. The tower is a carefully carved form that rises from a broad base alive with pedestrian activity, commerce, and transport, serving a newly renovated Staten Island Ferry Terminal and the landmark Battery Maritime Building. The generous public space at the building's base would accommodate the nearly 100,000 ferry and subway commuters that pass through the station each hour during morning and evening commutes, with a public park and broad esplanades overlooking the harbor.

From this multifaceted base, the rose-gray granite shaft ascends with modest setbacks and chamfered corners, reducing the tower's apparent mass. Near the top, the shaft is crowned with an octagonal drum, upon which sit three glass domes of diminishing sizes, with a communication spire at the apex. Public restaurants and an observation deck on the 55th floor enliven the building's top with pedestrian activity and provide panoramic views of the city and its waterfront, including the Statue of Liberty.

The real estate market stalled the completion of this project, but the building stands as a cogent reminder that great cities have always had memorable waterfronts. South Ferry Plaza would reclaim that distinction for New York.

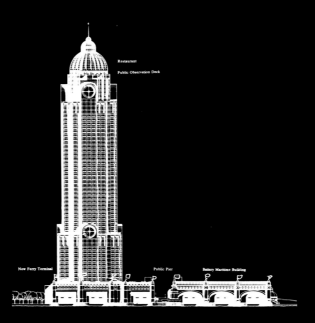

East Elevation

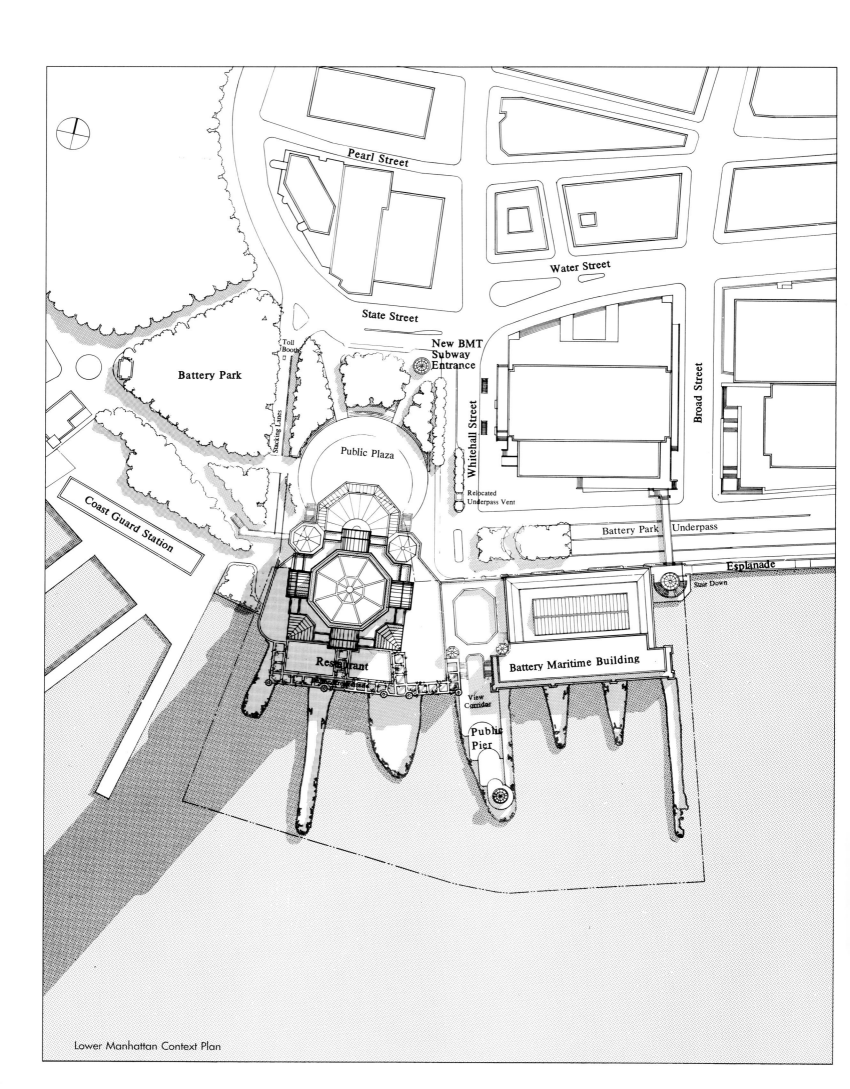

Pearl Street

Water Street

State Street

New BMT
Subway
Entrance

Battery Park

Toll
Booth

Stacking Lanes

Whitehall Street

Broad Street

Public Plaza

Relocated
Underpass Vent

Coast Guard Station

Battery Park Underpass

Esplanade

Stair Down

Restaurant

Battery Maritime Building

View
Corridor

Public
Pier

Lower Manhattan Context Plan

Previous Spread: Tower as it fits into lower Manhattan waterfront context.

Left: Ferry terminal forms the base from which the office tower grows.

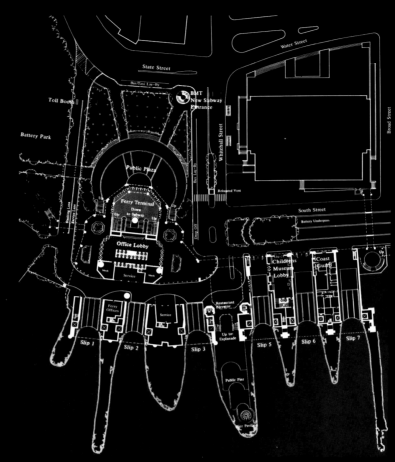

Grade Level Plan

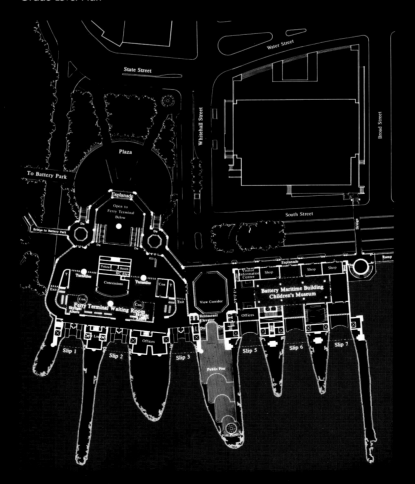

Mezzanine Level Plan

Top: Tower is an inspiring landmark and beacon in lower Manhattan.

Center: Office tower opens to a new public plaza.

Bottom: Tower entrance faces onto new public plaza.

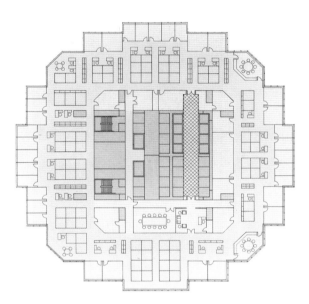

Typical Base Office Floor Plan

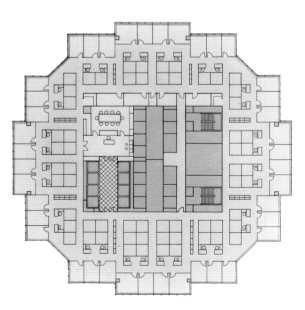

Typical Tower Office Floor Plan

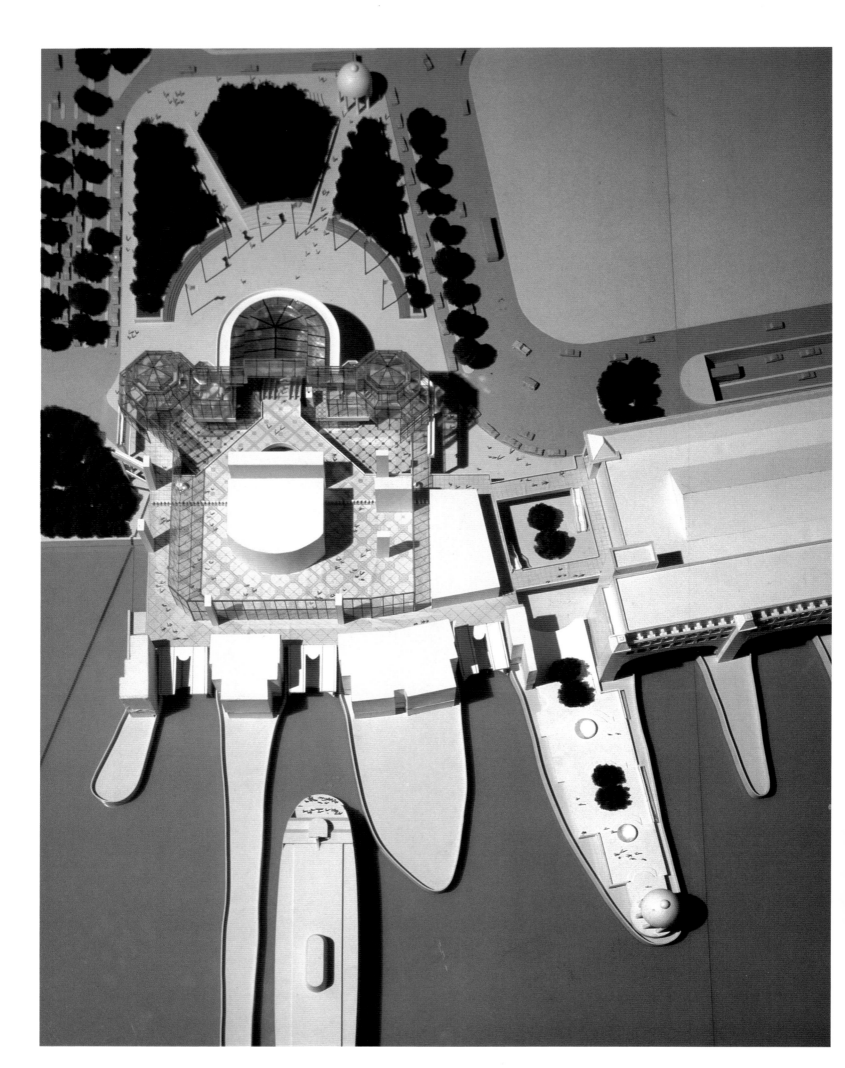

Opposite Page: Model
of new Staten Island
Ferry Terminal shows its
relationship with boats
and public plaza.

Left: Rendering from
the Hudson River.

121

WATTANA PLACE

BANGKOK, THAILAND

The site for this fifty-story residential complex is in the center of the new office district of Bangkok. The program called for a variety of condominium residences designed for young professional couples, executives, and others who want to be within walking distance of their working environment, restaurants, schools, and shopping areas.

At the street level Wattana Place has a number of amenities that serve both the residents and the neighborhood. The building's six-story base is devoted to on-site parking for 286 cars, restaurants, shopping, and a conference center offering generous meeting facilities. As the base extends toward the major thoroughfare, its top story and roof contain a health club

and a swimming pool—welcome amenities in Bangkok. Out of the base rises the residential tower, with 252 condominiums that have spectacular panoramic views. The tower's stepped profile mediates the building's scale between the skyline and the street and enhances views with bay windows that step out at each residential unit.

The bay windows provide floor-to-ceiling glass, which increases the spaciousness of each residence. This "inner wall" of the tower is protected by an outer wall of balconies that provide welcome shade in the humid, tropical climate. The balconies also encourage cross-ventilation and natural cooling of the residences.

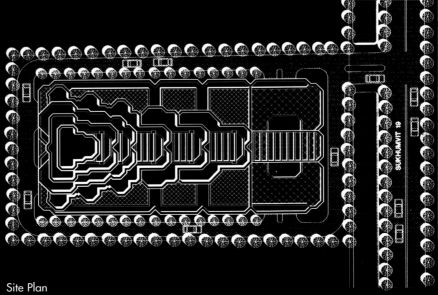

Site Plan

Previous Page: Building
has a towering presence
on the main thoroughfare.

Top: Building cascades in
a series of setbacks to the
street.

Center: Terraces at the
numerous setbacks are
shaded by trellises
overhead.

Bottom: Building's glass is
shaded by balconies that
mitigate heat gain.

Opposite Page: At night,
building rises gracefully
to become a beacon on
the skyline.

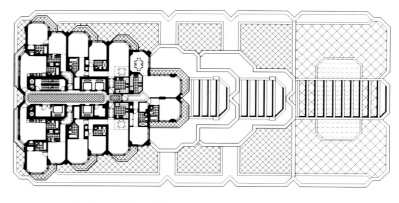

Upper Level Residential Floor Plan

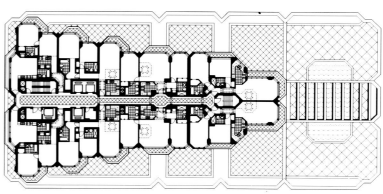

Lower Level Residential Floor Plan

THE VANDERBILT

NEW YORK, NEW YORK

The challenge in the design of the Vanderbilt residential complex was to provide comfortable condominium residences for young couples and families who enjoy living in midtown Manhattan, within walking distance of their work. Occupying a site between 40th and 41st Street on New York's East Side, The Vanderbilt rises above its dense urban context with apartments that offer light, views, and air.

Entry to the forty-two-story tower is found on East 40th Street, through a green public plaza with fountains, designed by Paul Friedberg. The stepped plan gives the tower a strong vertical profile, accentuating the building's height by articulating its vertical elements. For example, the corner terraces on the south elevation give The Vanderbilt the appearance of three engaged towers, which helps modulate the scale. The exterior materials are brick with concrete slab balconies, faithful to the city's palette of masonry buildings. The stepped plan also adds

structural strength. The Vanderbilt's below-grade levels contain an Olympic-sized pool, a health spa, laundry facilities, and parking. The entry level offers a gracious lobby and a restaurant, both of which can be easily accessed from the through block driveway between East 40th and East 41st Street.

The Vanderbilt's 370 condominium residences range in size from studios to two-bedrooms, with penthouse apartments that offer the ability to combine apartments so that you can have larger four-bedroom residences. On the south side, the tower's stepped profile opens apartments to sunlight and terrace views west of downtown, while the north side steps back for vistas of midtown. East-side units have overlooks to the East River, while the full floor-to-ceiling window walls give the apartments a feeling of spaciousness. New York has a long tradition of distinctive residential buildings, and The Vanderbilt fits well into that historical context, adding to the mix of midtown living.

Typical Floor Plan

Previous Page: Tower steps back on the south side, welcoming sunlight, views, and providing privacy.

Top: Glassy walls give the building its ethereal quality at night.

Center: Model of the tower accentuates its vertical emphasis.

Bottom: Generous motor court provides for vehicular service and drop-off.

Opposite Page: At the tower's base, a landscaped park provides a welcome urban amenity for residents.

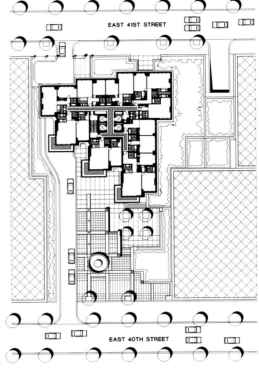

Typical Floor Plan

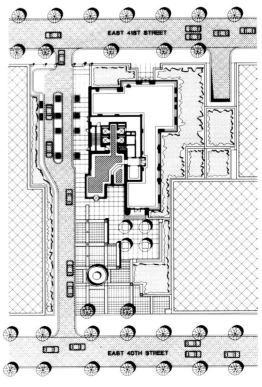

Ground Level Floor Plan

ST. RAPHAEL

NAPLES, FLORIDA

This luxury residential development in the Pelican Bay community of Naples capitalizes strongly on its unique site. The residential development occupies a space with the Gulf of Mexico to the west and a championship golf course to the east. The focus of the architectural design has been to capture the site's natural beauty and to give a variety of ways to live throughout the complex.

Fourteen private three-story villas, each with its own swimming pool, garden, and garage, comprise the base of the complex. Luxurious tower and penthouse residences with views of the Gulf and the golf course complement the villas. The richly appointed spaces

of a grand salon, billiard room, club room, board room, library, a private health club, a swimming pool, and tennis courts complete the public areas of the complex. To the north and south of the main public lobby and entrance are five garden residences with gracious, landscaped gardens and private swimming pools.

Frank Williams placed four pairs of elevators to serve two apartments per floor, which gives the St. Raphael a feeling of identity in the complex. Most of the 164 suite residences have views both east and west, which allows every resident to enjoy sunrises as well as sunsets.

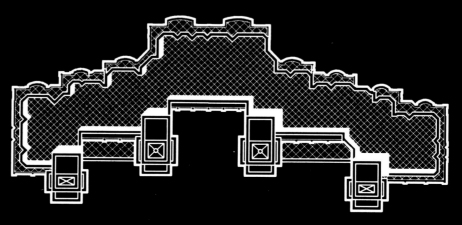

Roof Plan

Previous Page: Entrance to the complex is framed by a row of Villas, with residential towers beyond.

Top: Architectural details, such as arches, are found in both the Villas and the residential towers.

Center: Crowns form the roofscape for the complex.

Bottom: At the residential tower tops are penthouses with wrap-around terraces.

Opposite Page: Complex combines residential towers with small-scale Villas.

Top: Architectural details, such as arches, are found in both the Villas and the towers.

Center: Each Villa unit can be entered from the front, where entrance garages are located.

Bottom: Villas each have a private pool in the rear yard.

Opposite Page: Low-scale Villas provide another way of living throughout the complex.

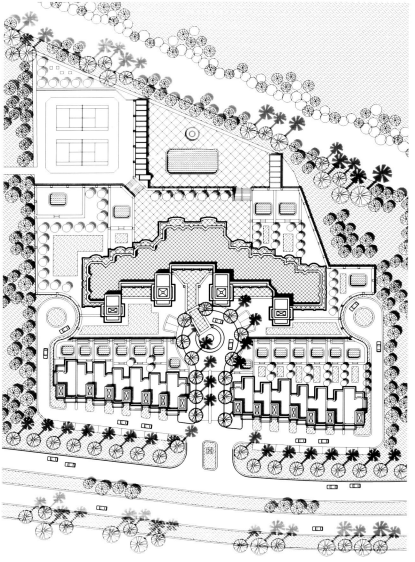

Site Plan

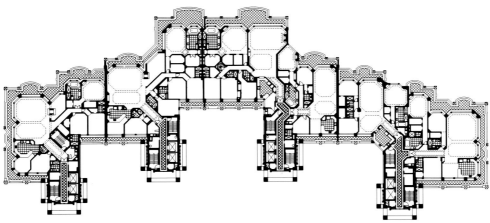

Penthouse Plans

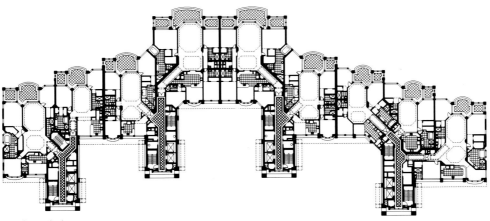

Typical Level Plans

YUNG RESIDENCE

HAWAII

This vacation house was designed for a client from Hong Kong whose mandate was that it should provide a maximum of enjoyment of the climate and views, with privacy. The oceanfront site gently slopes toward the beach, from which issue prevailing breezes. The client is a collector of antique cars who also enjoys outdoor cooking and entertaining. The 7,000-square-foot house is conceived of as a series of outdoor pavilions that step back from the beach.

The concept is to open the vacation residence to view the ocean and close off all openings along the side yards to maximize privacy.

Sympathetic to its ocean-front setting, the house virtually disappears beneath the roof terraces, trellises, and the pool. In the Yung residence, there is a variety of outdoor living spaces. Some to the east and west edges are small and intimate; others are large, designed for outdoor cooking, and offer panoramic views of the ocean.

One circulates through the terrace levels via open-air stairs. The concrete trellises overhead give the house a delicate texture, provide passive cooling, and filter the sunlight. This great waterfront house is a pavilion for tropical living.

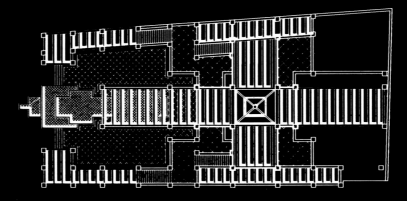

Roof Plan

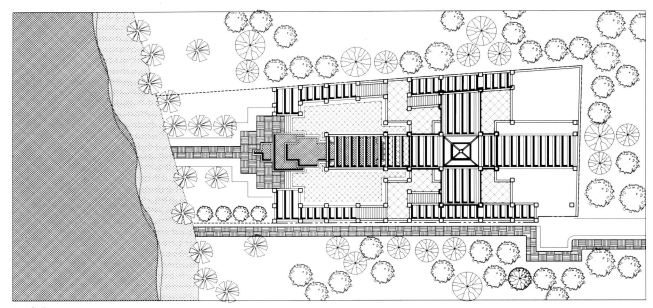

Roof Plan

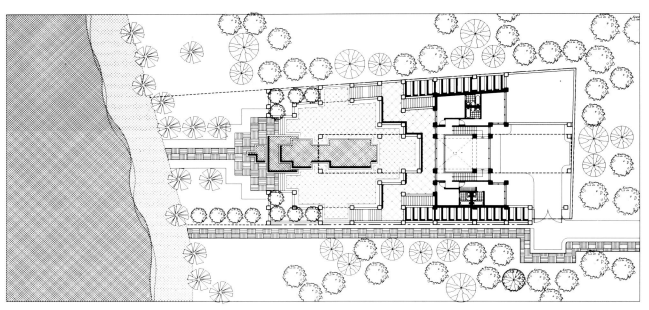

Upper Level Plan

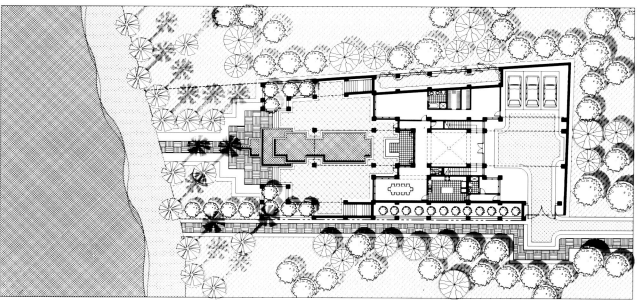

Ground Level Plan

Previous Spread: House's scale is in keeping with the island's delicate vernacular buildings.

Top: Trelises provide shade for the main recreation area.

Center: Sides of the house have no windows to maintain privacy.

Bottom: Trellises shade both terraces and a pool on lower level.

Following Spread: Plan of the house, as expressed outside, is a cruciform with trellises to filter light.

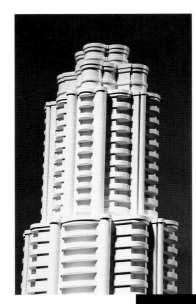

LANG SUAN PLACE

BANGKOK, THAILAND

This 142-condominium residential building—sited not far from another Frank Williams project, Lang Suan Ville—faces a precinct of embassies for the United States, Britain, and New Zealand. The buildings are surrounded by lush, shady parks, and Lang Suan Place's proximity to this open green area accentuates its towering form and is one of its primary amenities.

This residential building with its stepped profile, generous balconies, and operable bay windows is welcome in this year-round tropical climate. The fourty-story tower is romantic in its curvilinear forms, and its streamlined shape is accented with deep shadow lines. Lang Suan Place also contains a number of amenities that are important in Bangkok residential buildings, such as a health spa and club, on-site parking for 182 cars, and a variety of meeting rooms.

Lang Suan Place features a two-layer exterior that provides shading for cooling and protection from the sun's glare. In the apartments, living rooms are located at the corners with generous views, light, and cross-ventilation. The curved balconies offer a shady respite on blistering hot days and help to passively cool the building. A plethora of rooftop gardens, overhead trellises, and swimming pools also provides great response to the climate. The building is constructed of a concrete frame over which is a beige tile exterior with a precision matte finish.

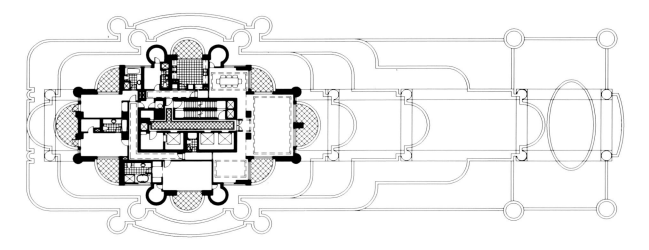

Typical Penthouse Floor Plan

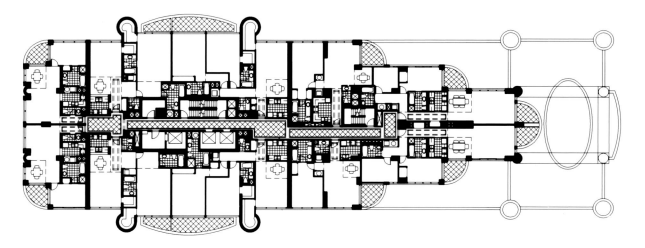

Typical Residential Floor Plan

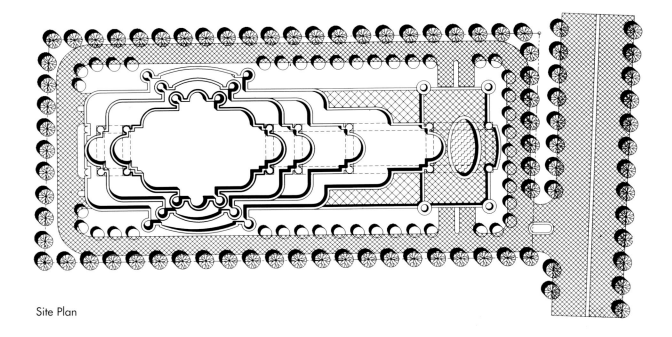

Site Plan

Previous Spread: Tower steps up from a pool on the lowest roof level.

Left: Building steps back from the main thoroughfare with strong vertical lines.

TRUMP PARC
NEW YORK, NEW YORK

Frank Williams's numerous projects around the world share a spirit of place that grows from his understanding of a city's architecture. In New York, his design for Trump Parc allowed him to rebuild a structure that is part of the same New York tradition that influences so many of his own new buildings in Manhattan.

Trump Parc occupies one of the most prestigious sites in the city: Central Park South, at virtually the midpoint of the Park's southern boundary. From this vantage, Frederick Law Olmsted's oasis in the city stretches to the north, east, and west like a verdant blanket. The building was designed by Murgatroyd & Ogden Architects and constructed in 1930 as the Barbizon Plaza, a hotel of exuberant Art Deco style. The rooms were large, and the hotel originally catered to musicians and world-class travelers. Over the years the Barbizon fell on hard times. Its rebirth as a residential building allowed its Deco features to be refurbished and its interior to be completely rebuilt to accommodate 350 new apartments. The building's entry was redesigned to take advantage of Central Park. Previously the hotel's front door was on 58th Street. The new design moves the entrance to Central Park South.

The exterior of the building was cleaned, new windows were installed, and its Deco ornamentation was gilded. Where the building steps back, garden terraces are provided. At the very top, Trump Parc's gilded crown is extended to conceal mechanical equipment and to enhance the building's silhouette on the skyline.

Typical Residential Floor Plan

Previous Page: Building, shown from Central Park, rises on its southern boundary.

Top: Existing building overlooks the breadth of Central Park.

Center: Model shows how building base wraps around corner, with tower growing from center.

Bottom: Building, shown from Central Park, rises on its southern boundary.

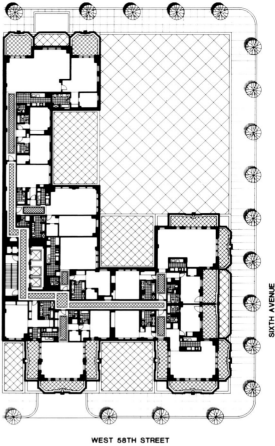

Typical Residential Floor Plan

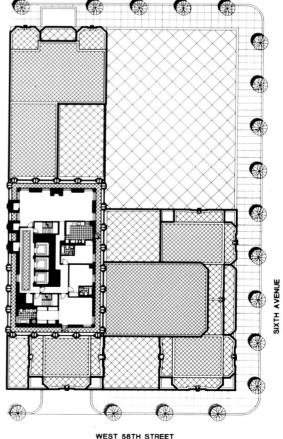

Typical Penthouse Floor Plan

Left: Model shows how building base wraps around corner, with tower growing from center.

TAJ MAHAL RESIDENTIAL TOWER

BOMBAY, INDIA

As India becomes a player in the international marketplace, its major cities have become destinations for investors from around the world. The Taj Mahal Residential Tower is designed to accommodate a worldly clientele, especially those who plan an extended stay. Located near the center of Bombay, the residental tower occupies a site with water views in two directions and is not far from the grand colonial hotel of the same name.

The residential tower, which contains 220 service apartments, takes the form of a twin-towered block with a long row of three-story villas running northerly. The villas provide accommodations in town-house fashion, with private garages directly off the street, terraces that offer welcoming breezes, and arched windows that recall a common element of Bombay's architecture. The twin towers, with their sculptural spires festooned with lights, create a landmark on the Bombay skyline, reminiscent of the old hotel's ornate profile and domed top. Because of Bombay's tropical climate, the Taj Mahal Residential Tower is designed with double walls to mitigate the heat and humidity. The first layer is made up of balconies and verandas that shade the building, providing passive cooling. The second layer of glass protects the building from rain. The towers' configuration allows no more than four apartments on each floor, which encourages a sense of privacy and security. The tower's top three floors feature single apartments with gracious balconies. All of the apartments are furnished, complete with phones, faxes, and other amenities that allow them to be used as a base of business operations. A restaurant at the ground level caters to a global variety of palates. Through its scale, materials, and memorable presence, the Taj Mahal Residential Tower communicates a sense of permanence and urban sophistication.

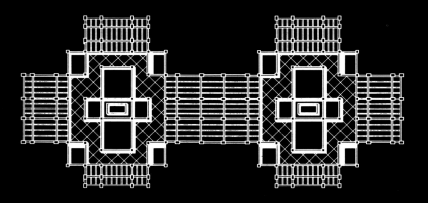

Roof Plan

Previous Page: Southeast view of residential tower.

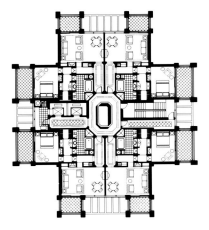

Typical Floor Plan

East Elevation

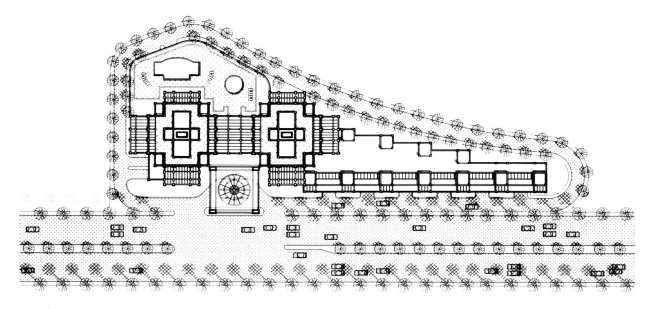

Site Plan

Top: Towers are punctuated with lanterns that mark it on the skyline.

Center: The base of the complex relates to the existing fabric of Bombay.

Bottom: The health club is located on top of the parking garage.

THE COLUMBIA
NEW YORK, NEW YORK

This 320-condominium residential building occupies a prominent corner site at Broadway and West 96th Street and is carefully calibrated to fit into the scale of this existing context. The building is not far from the university for which it is named; its most active edge lies along Broadway, with a ground floor filled with shops and restaurants. On Broadway, The Columbia presents a strong, fifteen-story wall with balconies articulated at the corners. This block blends with the scale of nearby buildings and is sympathetic to the context with its materials of brick and glass. At the top of this block is a large band of floor-to-ceiling windows, which marks the location of a health club and meeting rooms.

Behind the slab along Broadway, set back into the site, The Columbia rises to its full height. The thirty-two-story structure is defined as a series of overlapping horizontal elements, with balconies thrusting out to capture views and fresh air. To break down the building's scale, the overlapping balconies slip past each other on each floor, creating a two-story-high external space that lets light into the living space. At the tower's core, a vertical shaft with corner windows extends toward Broadway, containing the building's elevators and unifying the complex.

The Columbia's lobby is entered from 96th Street. This space is distinguished by its two-story height, clean lines, and natural light. The lobby's material palette is dominated by the same brick that is used on the exterior. Not only does this tie the inside to the outside, but the interior masonry gives The Columbia a strong sense of permanence.

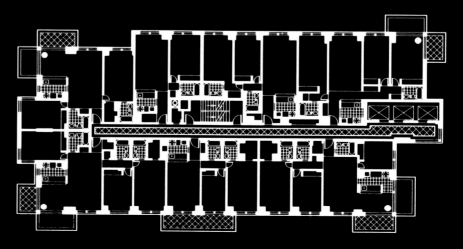

Typical Floor Plan

Previous Page: Building's vigorous balconies give it a sculptural quality.

Top: Broadway elevation has a street wall in scale with many of the existing buildings along Broadway.

Center: Street level entrance along West 96th Street.

Bottom: The corner view of 96th Street and Broadway.

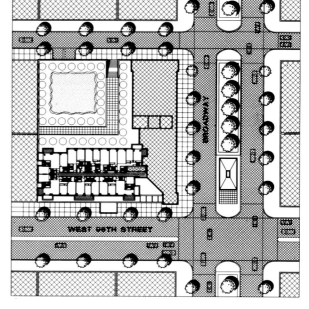

Upper Level Plan

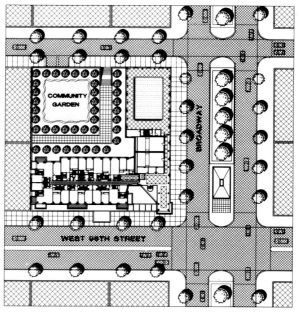

Lower Level Plan

Left: Tower and base of
building are held together
by strong vertical elements.

THE ALEXANDRIA

NEW YORK, NEW YORK

Many of New York's important residential buildings on the city's Upper West Side are noted for their distinctive roofscapes. These include The Dorilton, a Second Empire structure at 71st Street and Broadway, and The Ansonia, a landmark with twin corner turrets piled high with classical ornamentation. The Alexandria shares the same block along Broadway with The Ansonia, and it is sympathetic to the older building in its distinctive profile, materials, and celebrated corner, topped with a glowing lantern.

The Alexandria is respectful of its context and tries to respond to this important corner in scale and spirit. The sloped-profile building contains 202 condominium apartments; the first three floors are contained within a classically inspired plinth that gives the building a solid foundation. This base also melds The Alexandria into the Broadway streetscape with its vibrant retail activity. The next dozen stories are articulated in a fashion similar to the apartment buildings of the past, with alternating bay windows and recessed balconies. The brick walls have

punched rectangular windows—common in New York buildings—and communicate a sense of solidity. At the corner is a turret-like element with balconies, which echoes in scale and spirit the architecture of the nearby Ansonia.

At its sixteenth story and above, each floor steps back eight feet, creating a gently sloped profile and open-air terraces that wrap the 72nd Street and Broadway façades. The resulting profile suggests the mansard roofs of The Ansonia. The definition of the bays is carried up through these setback floors, while the gracious terraces provide views of the neighborhood and nearby parks. At the top of the twenty-four-story building is a glazed octagonal mechanical penthouse, which is The Alexandria's beacon on Broadway.

New York's grand apartment houses are distinctive in their human scale, classical proportion, and urban amenity—all qualities that make The Alexandria part of this tradition.

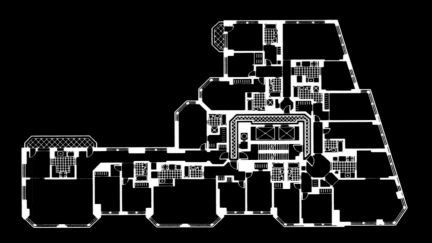

Typical Floor Plan

Previous Page: Corner is celebrated with a vertical element that helps turn the building and relates to Ansonia.

Top: Vertical bay windows on the façade stress the building's height.

Center: Building's base is a two-story band that contains retail and commercial space.

Bottom: At night, rooftop penthouse becomes a beacon of light on Broadway.

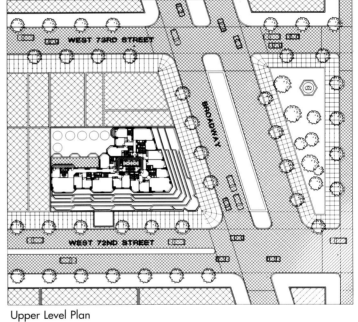

Upper Level Plan

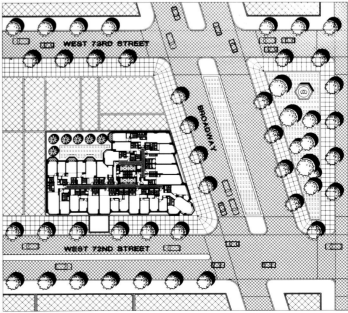

Lower Level Plan

Left: Terraced roof mitigates the building's scale in the neighborhood.

Left: At corner of Broadway and 72nd Street, building is shown in its contextual relationship with Ansonia.

THE BELAIRE

NEW YORK, NEW YORK

The Belaire is a unique expression of a partnership in which a major hospital and a major real estate developer worked together to create a single building, designed to accommodate their differing needs. The site lies between East 71st and 72nd Streets, at the cul-de-sac overlooking the East River, FDR Drive, and Roosevelt Island. New York's Hospital for Special Surgery owned the site and was in need of additional space for sports medicine facilities, administrative offices, and nurses' residences. In exchange for the land, the Zeckendorf Company agreed to build the needed hospital facilities, with 190 private condominium residences above. The design challenge was to meld the two uses into a unified building.

The solution is an ingenious combination that takes advantage of a difficult site that rises three stories from 71st to 72nd Street. The hospital space occupying the first fourteen stories is entered from 71st Street through a large welcoming plaza. Above the first fourteen floors are twenty-five stories of condominium residences with a lobby on 72nd Street. The Belaire's two programs are served by different elevator banks. On the 71st Street side the building steps out with floor-to-ceiling bay windows to accentuate views of the river to the southeast, while also maximizing sunlight in these spaces. On the 72nd Street elevation, the building steps back east and west to afford river views and vistas of upper Manhattan. The bay windows on the southerly side give the tower its vertical thrust and tie it to the traditional architecture of New York in the 1920s and 1930s. The top five stories are sculpted to give the building a crown, with penthouse apartments that feature wrap-around terraces. The brick exterior is part of New York's building tradition, and the change in surface texture and window treatment above the fourteenth floor marks the dividing line between The Belaire's two unique functions.

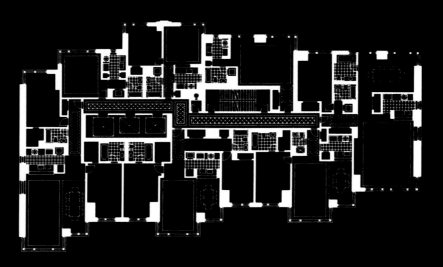

Typical Floor Plan

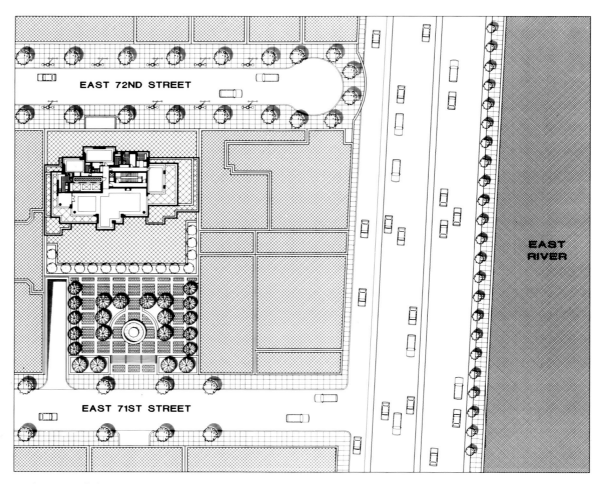

Penthouse Level Plan

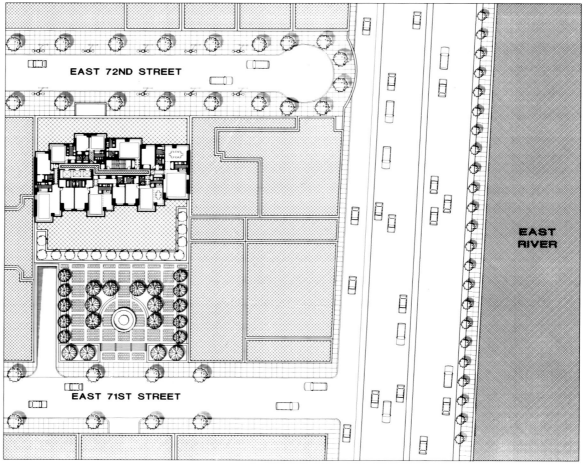

Lower Level Plan

Previous Spread: From across the East River, The Belaire rises on the Manhattan skyline.

Left: Seventy-first Street entrance plaza is defined by tower and flanking buildings.

Opposite Page: As sun rakes across its surface, tower expresses its sculptural quality.

Left: Building allows views of FDR Drive and the East River.

CHENGDU RESIDENTIAL COMMUNITY
CHENGDU, CHINA

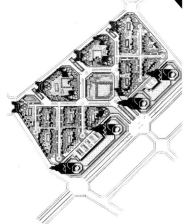

Traditional concepts of Chinese courtyard housing were adapted in the design of this master plan. The resulting design is a neighborhood complex which includes 2,500 residential apartments, shopping, schools, community facilities, and public open spaces for sports, recreation, playgrounds, and parking facilities.

The architectural design is based on the traditional Chinese courtyard housing found in the city of Chengdu and many other Chinese cities. The indigenous housing is low-rise, high-density, and punctuated with open courtyards through which residents pass to and from their homes. This prototype serves as the basis for the new development in order to create a comfortable residential scale and to enhance the sense of permanence for the community. The courtyards in the new community are the organizing element of the plan and are sized and proportioned similarly to the vernacular. The result is multi-use

space with various options and functions found throughout the expansive site.

The residential units are combined both vertically and horizontally to create a wide variety of low-rise (two- to four-story walkups) and mid-rise (fourteen- to eighteen-story residential buildings. Residences are clustered in densities similar to the traditional Chengdu communities. Bridges link the clusters, which contain a mix of functions, so that children can move safely from home to school without crossing a major roadway.

The system of construction is a modular design based on a "kit of parts." The kitchen and bathrooms are manufactured in a factory as contained units and dropped into place during construction. This development is an example of how a contemporary housing scheme can benefit from ancient and time-honored architectural typologies, while building with the latest technology.

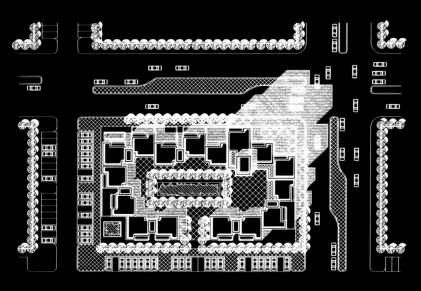

Typical Cluster Site Plan

Previous Page: Master plan offers housing at a variety of scales, based on traditional Chinese architecture.

Top: Bridges link clusters of housing and towers to shops and schools, providing safe travel for children.

Center: Vehicular traffic is bridged by pedestrian routes.

Bottom: Residential towers are surrounded by lower scale housing.

Opposite Page: Scale of the complex is similar to other residential neighborhoods in the city.

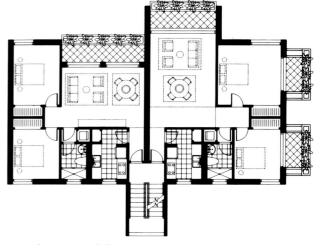

Typical Lower Level Plan

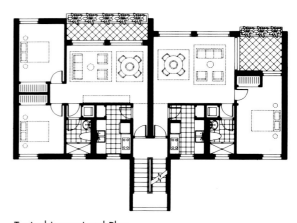

Typical Lower Level Plan

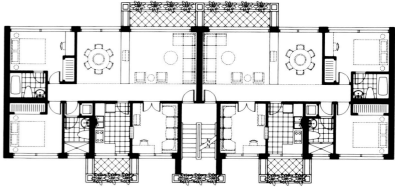

Typical Lower Level Plan

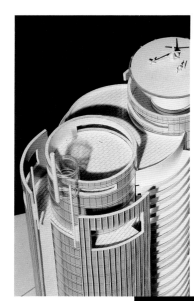

SATHORN INTERNATIONAL TOWER

BANGKOK, THAILAND

This thirty-story office building is programmed to handle all the various demands of state-of-the art international business activity. Sathorn International Tower is located on a corner site in a newly built-up office center of downtown Bangkok, not far from the Sukhothai Hotel. The tower is organized to serve both the neighborhood and the office tenants. On the lower levels there are a large health club, international shops, and restaurants. There is also parking for 200 cars. The upper stories contain 750,000 square feet of twenty-four-hour, state-of-the-art international office space. At the apex is a helicopter landing pad—a welcome amenity given the city's traffic.

While the immediate vicinity of this project is populated with boxy, minimal skyscrapers, this tower stands out due to its curvilinear geometry of converging cylinders. The central cylinder emphasizes the horizontal, while the flanking elements accentuate the vertical. Dividing the building into three cylinders breaks down its scale (as do the large voids at the top) and exaggerates the building's height and scale.

For climate control, the flanking cylinders have a screened curtain wall that filters sunlight, while the central cylinder's curved balconies provide shade and cooling breezes in this humid, tropical climate.

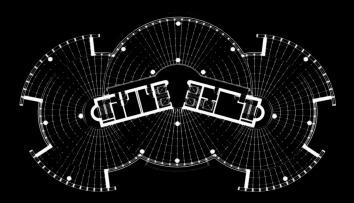

High-Rise Office Plan

Previous Page: Center cylinder is organized as a "zipper" to unite the cylinders on either side.

Top: Large-scale openings at the top break down the building's scale.

Center: Office building's form is articulated in a series of horizontal elements.

Bottom: Site plan provides open space around the towers for office workers.

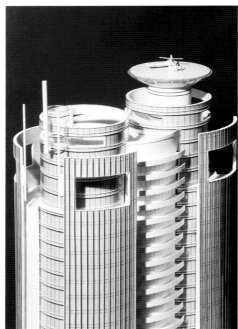

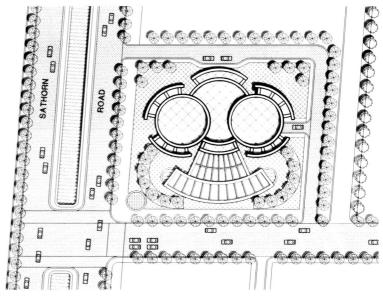

Site Plan

Left: Office building provides a helicopter pad at the summit.

St. Laurent

Naples, Florida

The St. Laurent is located in the Waterpark Place community of Pelican Bay, which commands spectacular views of the Gulf of Mexico to the west and the championship golf course of Pelican Bay to the east. The site plan concept is a metaphor of the prow of a ship, pointed toward the Gulf. The building contains 105 residences, ranging in size from two to three bedrooms. On every floor, elevator cores serve two or three suites, which gives The St. Laurent great privacy and makes it feel like a small community with great identity. The building's chevron form gives all of the residents privacy, while at the same time opening unparalleled views of the water and golf course. Curved balconies to the west provide shade and welcome breezes.

On the ground floor the public amenities include the lobby, grand foyer, board room, library, health club, billiard room, and guest suites for the residents' use. The lush tropical landscaping of The St. Laurent is complemented by the outside public amenities of the swimming pool, whirlpool spa, tennis courts, and enclosed parking garage. The building's exterior emphasizes the vertical elements, such as piers, pilasters and bay windows, giving The St. Laurent a stature that belies its twenty-two stories.

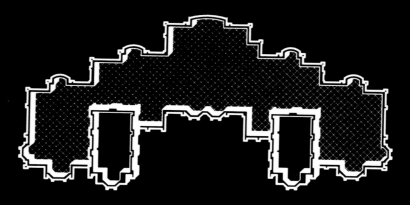

Roof Plan

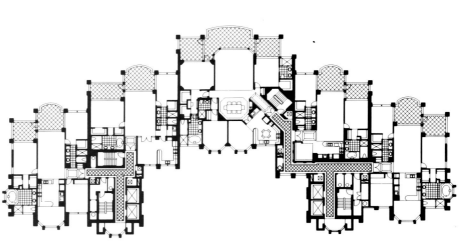

Typical Floor Plan

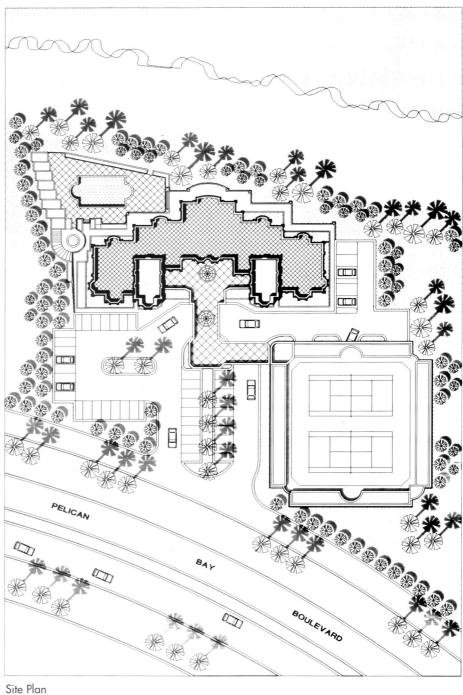

PELICAN

BAY

BOULEVARD

Site Plan

Top: Elevator cores of the building have bay windows to provide light.

Center: Elevator cores are crowned with glass and provide a focal point.

Bottom: Vertical elements of the tower are the bay windows.

CHIRATHIVAT RESIDENCE & ART GALLERY

BANGKOK, THAILAND

The architectural design of this urban residence in the heart of the thriving Asian city of Bangkok was a challenge due to its unique program. The clients are great collectors of art. With an extensive collection of Modern and Contemporary art, they established the Kyoko Chirathivat Art Gallery. Thus, the house serves as a cultural center in the city as well as a private residence.

The incorporation of the gallery on the ground floor called for the architectural program to fulfill two functions: public spaces to accommodate visitors to the art gallery, and private spaces to meet the living requirements of the clients. Conceptually, the gallery commands the ground floor, while the private residence is organized on the upper two levels. With the vertical separation of the public and private realms, the residence balances the public needs of the art gallery and the privacy desired for the residence. Within the residence, the living and dining rooms are organized on the second level, with the bedrooms and study devoted to the third floor and a swimming pool next to the bedrooms. The proportions of the art gallery and the living/dining rooms make these spaces perfect for entertaining.

Through the collaboration of a local architect, a world-class lighting consultant from London, and an international interior designer in Paris, a gracious urban residence has been created that maintains the privacy of the residents, but allows public space for lavish entertaining during art openings.

View into Dinning Room

Previous Page: Urban residence has a combination of terraces and a swimming pool on the top levels.

Top: Entrance court allows for patrons to be dropped off during art gallery openings, as well as serving the residence.

Bottom: Pool is accessible directly from the third floor master bedroom and has trellis to filter light.

Top: Trellis over swimming pool provides shade from the sun.

Center: View of outdoor garden terrace to pool area.

Bottom: View of swimming pool toward private library and reading room.

Right: Living room is designed for entertaining and to display part of the art collection.

CREDITS

Principals and staff members
who have collaborated on
the buildings and projects in
this book.

PRINCIPALS
Frank Williams
SENIOR ASSOCIATES
Veronica Garaycochea-Williams
Robert Laudenschlager
ASSOCIATES
Alok Anil
Mohamed Yakub

FORMER ASSOCIATES
Lawrence Adams
Richard Kotz
Steve Rothman
Frank Uellendahl
Paula Wisnik
STAFF
Kika Adler
Frank Alcok
Basel Aleraf
Janette Alexander
Carol Anderson
Celia Apalategun
Steven Arroyo
Albert Ascalon
Robert Ashton
Maria Asteinza
Tim Aziz
Cecil Baklor
Stephanie Barnett
James Belluardo
Marco Benjamin
John P. Bohan
Mary Brodus
Ross Cann
Hong Chang-Lin
Richard Charlson
Nora Coffey
Rogers Cooper
Zheng Dai
Victoria Davidson
Douglas R. Disbrow
Anthony Dokanovitch
Marjann Dumoulein
Jori Erdman
Valerie Feinberg
Ronald Frankel
Babette Freson
Dee Gale
Joseph Galea
Andrea Galecovic-Vujovic
Yana Gorokhovskaya
Hunter Greene
Janet Grubb
Joseph Hand
Milton James
Vladimir Kaushansky

David L. King
Tomas Klopsch
Arthur Knapp
Lester Korzilius
Giles Laheurte
John Lam
Robert Lane
Rosanna Lee
Tracy Leipold
Robert Levy
Kathryn Linder
Betty Liu
Peter Locascio
Ramon Lopez
Steven Margolis
Marian McGee
Monty Mitchell
Noha Nakib
Suzanne O'Donnell
John Ostlund
Sam Packard
Sherida Paulsen
Roy Pertchek
Cliff L. Peterson
Jason Popkin
Kevin Preuiett
Bryan Price
Christopher Riedner
Alan Robinson
Victor Rodriguez
Nenad Rukavina
Carlos Sainz
Ingrid Salcedo
Rosie Salcedo
Richard Schneebeli
Michael Selditch
Les Schmerzler
Brooks Slocum
John Sokol
James C. Stevens
Jessica Stewart
Christopher Stienon
Michel St. Pierre
Patricia E. Supplee
Stephen Terr
Carrow Thibault
Franklin Tomaselli
Thomas Tow
Neil Troiano
William Van Horn
Trish Vevera
Francisco Villanueva
Nicola Walter
Christopher Werner
Eileen White
David Williams
Josefa Witteman
Barbara Ann Wolf
Alfie Woods
Debra Workman
Khozaim Zakavi
Andrea Zimmerman

THE RIHGA ROYAL HOTEL
NEW YORK, NEW YORK
OWNER: International Hotel Group
Associates, Osaka, Japan
PROGRAM: 514 all-suite hotel, restaurants,
lobby lounge, meeting rooms, banquet
facilities, health spa.
ARCHITECT: Frank Williams & Associates,
Architects, New York, New York
INTERIOR DESIGN: Birch Coffey Design
Associates, New York, New York; Marcel
Bequillard Interior Design; New York, New York
PHOTOGRAPHS: Jeff Goldberg/Esto;
Wolfgang Hoyt/Esto; Peter Paige; David
Williams/3D Media; Mohamed Yakub/Frank
Williams & Associates
MODELS: George Machalani Architectural
Models

WORLD WIDE PLAZA
NEW YORK, NEW YORK
OWNER: The Zeckendorf Company,
New York, New York; The K. G. Land Company
New York, New York; World-Wide Holdings
Corporation, New York, New York; Arthur G.
Cohen Properties Inc., New York, New York
PROGRAM: 2.5-million-square-foot mixed-use
office, 660 residential, shopping, theaters, and
parking for 450 cars. Frank Willliams &
Associates, Architects are the architects for the
residential complex, parking garage, health
club, and shops.
ARCHITECTS: Frank Williams & Associates,
Architects—residential building, New York,
New York; Skidmore, Owings & Merrill,
Architects—commercial building,
New York, New York
INTERIOR DESIGN: Pilat & Davis, Architects,
New York, New York
PHOTOGRAPHS: Veronica Garaycochea-
Williams/Frank Williams & Associates;
Jeff Goldberg/Esto; Elizabeth Jones/Lenscape
MODELS: Architectural Dimensions
RENDERINGS: Michael McCann

SHANGHAI INTERNATIONAL PLAZA
SHANGHAI, CHINA
OWNER: SITICO-Shanghai International Trust
& Investment Corp., Shanghai, China
PROGRAM: Banking (200,000 square feet),
shopping (200,000 square feet), new office
building (1,000,000 square feet), new public
plaza, public observation level at top of build-
ing, restaurants.
ARCHITECT: Frank Williams & Associates,
Architects, New York, New York
STRUCTURAL ENGINEER: Cantor, Seinuk
Group, New York, New York

MECHANICAL ENGINEER: Jaros, Baum & Bolles, New York, New York
PHOTOGRAPHS: Veronica Garaycochea-Williams/Frank Williams & Associates; Mohamed Yakub/Frank Williams & Associates
MODELS: Awad Architectural Models

LANG SUAN VILLE
BANGKOK, THAILAND
OWNER DEVELOPMENT: Wave Development Ltd., Bangkok, Thailand
PROGRAM: 128 condominium residences, garden-terraced residences, health spa/club, swimming pool, 149-car parking garage, meeting rooms and offices.
ARCHITECTS: Frank Williams & Associates, Architects, New York, New York; Wave Architects Ltd., Bangkok, Thailand
INTERIOR DESIGN: Rirkrit and Associates, Bangkok, Thailand; Tsao & McKown Architects, New York, New York
LIGHTING DESIGN: Isometrix Lighting & Design, Ltd., London, England
PHOTOGRAPHS: Mohamed Yakub/Frank Williams & Associates
MODELS: George Machalani Architectural Models, Wave Development Company

THE BRITTANY
NAPLES, FLORIDA
OWNER: Gulf Bay Development, Inc., Naples, Florida
PROGRAM: 121 luxury condominium residences, six luxury residential villas, lobby-level public area, parking garage, swimming pool, cabanas, tennis courts, health spa, parking.
ASSOCIATED ARCHITECTS: Frank Williams & Associates, Architects, New York, New York; Architectural Network, Inc., Naples, Florida
INTERIOR DESIGN: Carole Korn Interiors, Naples, Florida
PHOTOGRAPHS: Flip Minott/Minott Motion Pictures; Veronica Garaycochea-Williams/Frank Williams & Associates
MODELS: George Machalani Architectural Models

WAVE INTERNATIONAL TOWER
BANGKOK, THAILAND
OWNER: Wave Development Ltd., Bangkok, Thailand
PROGRAM: 500,000-square-foot office building, shops and restaurant, meeting rooms, parking.
ARCHITECTS: Frank Williams & Associates, Architects, New York, New York; Wave Architects Ltd., Bangkok, Thailand
PHOTOGRAPHS: Mohamed Yakub/Frank Williams & Associates
MODELS: Awad Architectural Models

THE GOTHAM
NEW YORK, NEW YORK
OWNER: The Zeckendorf Company, New York, New York; Tobishima Associates, New York, New York; World-Wide Holdings, New York, New York
PROGRAM: 241 luxury condominium residences, cinemas, shopping at grade level, health club and pool.
ARCHITECT: Frank Williams & Associates, Architects, New York, New York
INTERIOR DESIGN: Pilat & Davis, Architects, New York, New York
PHOTOGRAPHS: Jeff Goldberg/Esto; Elizabeth Jones/Lenscape
MODELS: Architectural Dimensions

101 CALIFORNIA
SAN DIEGO, CALIFORNIA
OWNER: S. D. Malkin Properties, San Diego, California; Catellus Development Corporation, San Diego, California
PROGRAM: 200 condominium residences (tower & town houses), 25,000 square feet of commercial with two restaurants, health club, two-level parking garage below grade.
ARCHITECTS: Frank Williams & Associates, Architects, New York, New York; City Design, Architects, San Diego, California
PHOTOGRAPHS: Charles Smith
MODELS: A. P. M. Linda Kelly

TRUMP PALACE
NEW YORK, NEW YORK
OWNER: The Trump Organization, New York, New York
PROGRAM: 383 luxury condominium residences, shops, parking, public plaza.
ARCHITECT: Frank Williams & Associates, Architects, New York, New York
INTERIOR DESIGN: Zaniz and Jakobowski, New York, New York
PHOTOGRAPHS: Jock Pottle/Esto; Mohamed Yakub/Frank Williams & Associates
MODELS: Maloof Architectural Models
RENDERINGS: Howard & Associates

THE FOUR SEASONS HOTEL
NEW YORK, NEW YORK
OWNER: Lai Sun Development Co., Hong Kong, China; Four Seasons Hotels, Inc., Toronto, Canada
PROGRAM: 375 luxury hotel rooms, lobby lounge on East 57th Street, shops and three restaurants, meeting rooms, health spa.
ASSOCIATED ARCHITECTS: Frank Williams & Associates, Architects, New York, New York; Pei, Cobb, Freed & Partners, Architects, New York, New York

ARCHITECT OF RECORD: Frank Williams & Associates, Architects, New York, New York
INTERIOR DESIGN: Chhada Siembieda & Partners, Long Beach, California
PHOTOGRAPHS: Jeff Goldberg/Esto; Thorney Lieberman; Jock Pottle/Esto; Pete Seaward; Peter Vitale; Veronica Garaycochea-Williams/Frank Williams & Associates; Mohamed Yakub/Frank Williams & Associates
MODELS: Maloof Architectural Models

THE TERRACE
BANGKOK, THAILAND
OWNER: Wave Development Ltd., Bangkok, Thailand
PROGRAM: 88 luxury condominium residences, parking garage, health club, swimming pool at roof level.
ARCHITECTS: Frank Williams & Associates, Architects, New York, New York; Architects 49 Limited, Bangkok, Thailand
LIGHTING DESIGN: Isometrix Lighting & Design, Ltd., London, England
PHOTOGRAPHS: Jock Pottle/Esto; Mohamed Yakub/Frank Williams & Associates
MODELS: Awad Architectural Models
RENDERINGS: David Williams/3D Media

THE PARK BELVEDERE
NEW YORK, NEW YORK
OWNER: The Zeckendorf Company, New York, New York; World-Wide Holdings Corporation, New York, New York
PROGRAM: 155 condominium residences, shops at grade level.
ARCHITECT: Frank Williams & Associates, Architects, New York, New York
INTERIOR DESIGN: Frank Williams & Associates, Architects, New York, New York
PHOTOGRAPHS: Robert Cameron/Cameron & Co.; Veronica Garaycochea-Williams/Frank Williams & Associates; Wolfgang Hoyt/Esto; Mohamed Yakub/Frank Williams & Associates
MODELS: Maloof Architectural Models
RENDERINGS: Michael McCann

BERLIN FRIEDRICHSTRASSE
BERLIN, GERMANY
OWNER: Dumas Corporation, London, England; S. D. Malkin Properties, San Diego, California
PROGRAM: Three blocks of shopping, office, hotel, residential.
ASSOCIATED ARCHITECTS: Frank Williams & Associates, Architects, New York, New York; Moore Ruble Yudell, Architects, Los Angeles, California
PHOTOGRAPHS: John Taft
MODELS: Model Concepts

189

RENDERINGS: Doug Jamieson and Curtis
Woodhouse

THE REGENT HOTEL
THE REGENT RESIDENCES
SHANGHAI, CHINA
OWNER: Four Seasons°Regent, Toronto, Canada;
Shanghai International Tendering Co., Shanghai,
China; Christiani & Nielson, Bangkok, Thailand;
Salim Group, Jakarta, Indonesia; HRH Prince
Alwaleed, Riyadh, Saudi Arabia
PROGRAM: 400 luxury hotel rooms, 200 service
residences, lobby lounge, two restaurants, meet-
ing rooms, parking, health club, swimming pools.
ARCHITECT: Frank Williams & Associates,
Architects, New York, New York
STRUCTURAL ENGINEER: Cantor Seinuk Group
New York, New York
PHOTOGRAPHS: Mohamed Yakub/Frank
Williams & Associates
MODELS: Awad Architectural Models

SOUTH FERRY PLAZA
NEW YORK, NEW YORK
OWNER: The Zeckendorf Company, New York,
New York; K.G. Land Company, New York, New
York; World-Wide Holdings Corporation,
New York, New York; Continental Development
Group, Inc., New York, New York
PROGRAM: New office building (1,500,000
square feet), new Staten Island Ferry terminal,
new plaza and subway connection, rehabilitation
of landmark Battery Maritime Building.
ASSOCIATED ARCHITECTS: Frank Williams &
Associates, Architects, New York, New York;
Fox & Fowle, Architects, New York, New York
PROJECT DIRECTOR: Edith Fisher, The Zeckendorf
Company, New York, New York
URBAN DESIGN: Raquel Ramati Associates Inc.,
New York, New York
STRUCTURAL ENGINEER: Robertson, Fowler &
Associates, New York, New York
MECHANICAL ENGINEER: Cosentini Associates,
New York, New York
PHOTOGRAPHS: Dan Cornish; Wolfgang
Hoyt/Esto; Mohamed Yakub/Frank Williams &
Associates
MODELS: Frank Williams & Associates; Maloof
Architectural Models
RENDERINGS: Michael McCann

WATTANA PLACE
BANGKOK, THAILAND
OWNER: Wave Development Ltd., Bangkok,
Thailand
PROGRAM: 220 luxury condominium residences,
parking garage, health club, swimming pool.
ARCHITECTS: Frank Williams & Associates,

Architects, New York, New York; Leigh & Orange,
Bangkok, Thailand
INTERIOR DESIGN: Christian Liaigre, Paris, France
LIGHTING DESIGN: Isometrix Lighting & Design
Ltd., London, England
PHOTOGRAPHS: Mohamed Yakub/Frank
Williams & Associates
MODELS: Awad Architectural Models
RENDERINGS: David Williams/3D Media

THE VANDERBILT
NEW YORK, NEW YORK
OWNER: The Zeckendorf Company, New York,
New York; World-Wide Holdings Corporation,
New York, New York
PROGRAM: 375 condominium residences, shops.
ARCHITECT: Frank Williams & Associates,
Architects, New York, New York
INTERIOR DESIGN: Frank Williams & Associates,
Architects, New York, New York
PHOTOGRAPHS: Jeff Goldberg/Esto; Elizabeth
Jones/Lenscape
MODELS: Architectural Dimensions

ST. RAPHAEL
NAPLES, FLORIDA
OWNER: Gulf Bay Development, Inc.,
Naples, Florida
PROGRAM: 164 residential condominium suites,
14 luxury residential villas, lobby-level public
area, swimming pool, cabanas, tennis courts,
health club, parking garage.
ASSOCIATED ARCHITECTS: Frank Williams &
Associates, Architects, New York, New York;
Architectural Network Inc., Naples, Florida
PHOTOGRAPHS: Flip Minott/Minott Motion
Pictures; Jock Pottle/Esto
MODELS: Awad Architectural Models

THE YUNG RESIDENCE
HAWAII
OWNER: Mr. & Mrs. Robert Yung,
Hong Kong, China
PROGRAM: Residence, ocean view site, master
bedroom suites, guest bedroom suites, outdoor
cooking facility.
ARCHITECTS: Frank Williams & Associates,
Architects, New York, New York
INTERIOR DESIGN: Frank Williams & Associates,
Architects, New York, New York
PHOTOGRAPHS: Mohamed Yakub/Frank
Williams & Associates
MODELS: Awad Architectural Models

LANG SUAN PLACE
BANGKOK, THAILAND
OWNER: Wave Development Ltd.,
Bangkok, Thailand

PROGRAM: 142 condominium residences, gar-
den-terraced apartments, health spa/club, 182-
car parking garage, meeting rooms.
ARCHITECTS: Frank Williams & Associates,
Architects, New York, New York; Leigh & Orange
Architects, Bangkok, Thailand
INTERIOR DESIGN: Rirkrit and Associates,
Bangkok, Thailand
PHOTOGRAPHS: Mohamed Yakub/Frank
Williams & Associates
MODELS: George Machalani Architectural Models
RENDERINGS: Richard Baehr

TRUMP PARC
NEW YORK, NEW YORK
OWNER: The Trump Organization,
New York, New York
PROGRAM: Existing hotel (500,000 square feet),
rebuilt with 350 new condominium residences,
shops, parking.
ARCHITECT: Frank Williams & Associates,
Architects, New York, New York
INTERIOR DESIGN: Henry Conversano,
New York, New York
PHOTOGRAPHS: Veronica Garaycochea-
Williams/Frank Williams & Associates;
Wolfgang Hoyt/Esto; Mohamed Yakub/Frank
Williams & Associates
MODELS: George Machalani Architectural Models

TAJ MAHAL RESIDENTIAL TOWER
BOMBAY, INDIA
OWNER: The Indian Hotels Company Limited,
Bombay, India
PROGRAM: 220 service residences, parking,
health club, swimming pool.
ARCHITECT: Frank Williams & Associates,
Architects, New York, New York
PHOTOGRAPHS: Mohamed Yakub/Frank
Williams & Associates
MODELS: Awad Architectural Models

THE COLUMBIA
NEW YORK, NEW YORK
OWNER: The Zeckendorf Company
New York, New York
PROGRAM: 320 condominium residences, park-
ing garage, restaurant, shops, community garden.
ARCHITECTS: Liebman, Williams & Ellis,
New York, New York
ARCHITECT OF RECORD: Frank Williams &
Associates, Architects, New York, New York
INTERIOR DESIGN: Frank Williams & Associates,
Architects, New York, New York
PHOTOGRAPHS: Mohamed Yakub/Frank
Williams & Associates
RENDERINGS: Michael McCann

THE ALEXANDRIA
NEW YORK, NEW YORK
OWNER: The Zeckendorf Company, New York,
New York; Wien, Malkin & Bettex, New York,
New York
PROGRAM: 202 luxury condominum residences,
shops.
ARCHITECT: Frank Williams & Associates,
Architects, New York, New York
DESIGN CONSULTANTS: Skidmore Owings &
Merrill, New York, New York
PHOTOGRAPHS: Veronica Garaycochea-
Williams/Frank Williams & Associates; Jeff
Goldberg/Esto; Elizabeth Jones/Lenscape
MODELS: Architectural Dimensions
RENDERINGS: Robert Steele

THE BELAIRE
NEW YORK, NEW YORK
OWNER: The Zeckendorf Company, New York,
New York; Hospital for Special Surgery, New
York, New York; K.G. Land Company,
New York, New York; World-Wide Holding
Corporation, New York, New York
PROGRAM: Hospital for Special Surgery and
Sports Medicine, nurses' residences, offices, 190
luxury condominium residences, health club,
parking.
ARCHITECT: Frank Williams & Associates,
Architects, New York, New York
INTERIOR DESIGN: Birch Coffey Design
Associates, New York, New York
PHOTOGRAPHS: Veronica Garaycochea-
Williams/Frank Williams & Associates;
Jeff Goldberg/Esto; Elizabeth Jones/Lenscape
MODELS: Architectural Dimensions
RENDERINGS: Michael McCann

CHENGDU RESIDENTIAL COMMUNITY
CHENGDU, CHINA
DEVELOPER: The Pei Group, New York, New
York; The Zeckendorf Company, New York,
New York
PROGRAM: Neighborhood complex, shops,
2,500 residential units, three schools, hospital,
community center recreational facility, public parks.
ARCHITECT: Frank Williams & Associates,
Architects, New York, New York
INTERIOR DESIGN: Frank Williams & Associates,
Architects, New York, New York
PHOTOGRAPHS: Mohamed Yakub/Frank
Williams & Associates
MODELS: Frank Williams & Associates

SATHORN INTERNATIONAL TOWER
BANGKOK, THAILAND
OWNER: Wave Development Ltd., Bangkok,
Thailand

PROGRAM: Office building (700,000 square
feet), health club, shops, restaurant, parking.
ARCHITECTS: Frank Williams & Associates,
Architects, New York, New York; Wave Architects
Ltd., Bangkok, Thailand
PHOTOGRAPHS: Mohamed Yakub/Frank
Williams & Associates
MODELS: Frank Williams & Associates

ST. LAURENT
NAPLES, FLORIDA
OWNER: Gulf Bay Development Inc.,
Naples, Florida
PROGRAM: 105 luxury condominium residences,
lobby-level public area, swimming pool,
cabanas, tennis courts, health club, parking
garage.
ASSOCIATED ARCHITECTS: Frank Williams &
Associates, Architects, New York, New York;
Architectural Network Inc., Naples, Florida
INTERIOR DESIGN: Carol Korn Interiors,
Naples, Florida
PHOTOGRAPHS: Flip Minott/Minott
Motion Pictures
MODELS: George Machalani Architectural Models

THE CHIRATHIVAT RESIDENCE AND
ART GALLERY
BANGKOK, THAILAND
OWNER: Mr. and Mrs. Chirathivat,
Bangkok, Thailand
PROGRAM: Three-story private residence, art
gallery on ground floor, major living and dining
rooms on second level, bedrooms, study and
swimming pool on third level.
ARCHITECTS: Frank Williams & Associates,
Architects, New York, New York; Tandem
Architects, Bangkok, Thailand
INTERIOR DESIGN: Christian Liaigre, Paris,
France
LIGHTING DESIGN: Isometrix Lighting & Design
Ltd., London, England
PHOTOGRAPHS: Pascal Chevallier/Agence;
Mohamed Yakub/Frank Williams & Associates
MODELS: Frank Williams & Associates

ARCHITECT'S NOTES & ACKNOWLEDGMENTS

Right: Frank Williams & Associates, Architects: Mohamed Yakub, Robert Laudenschlager, Frank Williams, Veronica Garaycochea-Williams, Alok Anil

Our architectural practice has focused primarily on hotels, urban residential, and mixed-use commercial buildings in New York and around the globe. The firm is committed to providing excellence in design at all stages of completing a building.

Today we have structured our architectural firm to respond to the new globalism that has changed the way we were practicing architecture in the 1980s.

It is becoming clear that we, as architects, are learning much about context, climate, and how to build in various parts of the world. We now must make sure that these architectural design tools and principles are incorporated in our architectural commissions here in America, which is also part of the global community. There have been so many wonderful contributions to the successful outcome of this book. I want to express my profound appreciation to those special people who contributed so much of their time and knowledge to this publication. Starting with Rockport Publishers, I want to thank Rosalie Grattaroti for her support of the design and publication of this volume. Mike Crosbie has written an insightful and very powerful analysis expressing my architectural design philosophy and has successfully navigated this book through all the many levels of collaboration necessary for this publication.

Alexander Kouzmanoff, my great, lifelong friend, has clearly summarized my architecture and has added the final words to clearly update my most recent Asian-rim architectural projects.

Lucas H. Guerra has brilliantly organized the very complicated design of the book, working with the many definitive, beautiful photographs by Jeff Goldberg of Esto.

Veronica Garaycochea-Williams, my wife and senior associate, has been the person responsible for the overall concept and structure of this book. By finding the publisher, working closely with me on the photographic selection, and working with Lucas H. Guerra on the graphic design of the book, she has added her input, talents, and energies to this publication.

My senior associate, Robert Laudenschlager, with his managerial skills has organized the text, drawings, and photographs for the buildings in the book. My associate, Mohamed Yakub, has contributed greatly with his beautiful photography, while my associate Alok Anil contributed the outstanding computer drawings. I would also like to thank my former associates, all of whom contributed greatly to the architectural design in this publication.

The building and projects represented in this book truly are a collaboration with all of our wonderful clients.